Scotland

40 Coast and Country Walks

published by
pocket mountains ltd
The Old Church, Annanside,
Moffat DG10 9HB

ISBN: 978-1-907025-66-2

A catalogue record for this book is available from the British Library

Contains Ordnance Survey data © Crown copyright and database right 2018, supported by out of copyright mapping 1945-1961

Printed in Poland

Introduction

The most northerly of Britain's island groups, Shetland is so far removed from the rest of the UK that it usually appears as an inset on maps. This archipelago of around 300 islands and skerries lies as far north as St Petersburg or Anchorage, and is almost 1000km north of London but only 643km south of the Arctic Circle. Although relatively little known to those from outside the islands, Shetland is a magnificent terrain for walkers, especially those who love to explore and get away from the beaten track. The coastal walking here includes some of the finest in the country, with superb cliffs, towering sea stacks, caves and natural arches seemingly around every corner.

Added to this is Shetland's better known claim to fame for its spectacular seabird colonies – huge gannetries, moorland packed with Arctic and great skuas, Arctic terns in the more sheltered spots, and everyone's favourite – the puffins. The islands also enjoy a dense population of otters, many seals, and a chance to see killer whales or other giants of the deep.

Beyond all this natural grandeur, Shetland's history is fascinating, too. The archaeological attractions are much less known than those on Orkney, but sites such as Jarlshof have preserved remains from prehistory right up to more recent times. These include Iron Age villages, chambered cairns, Viking longhouses, Pictish carvings and circular stone Iron Age

towers, or brochs as they are known. The most impressive and complete of these in existence is on the island of Mousa.

Safety

Although most of these walks are termed moderate, much of Shetland is remote and many of the routes are pathless and can be rough underfoot. Choose sturdy footwear and carry waterproof clothing. The summary at the start of each walk should help you choose what will be appropriate. The sketch map accompanying every walk is meant as an outline guide rather than a navigational aid, so for all but the most straightforward routes an Ordnance Survey map is essential.

Access

Scotland has fantastic access rights, some of the most progressive in Europe, thanks to the Land Reform (Scotland) Act 2003. This gives walkers the right of access over most land away from residential buildings and gardens. It is balanced with a set of responsibilities set out in the Scottish Outdoor Access Code, full details of which can be found at www.outdooraccess-scotland.com, where there is also some useful advice on wild camping.

In Shetland sheep and cattle often graze on unfenced land or in fields along the route of walks, and ground-nesting birds are abundant; therefore, dogs must be kept under strict control, especially in spring and early summer and whenever livestock is present. Even an encounter with a friendly dog can cause a ewe to abort a lamb and there have been cases of sheep being driven over cliffs by free-running dogs. Keep well away from cows with calves if you have a dog.

Transport

Shetland is served by overnight vehicle ferries operating seven days a week between Aberdeen and Lerwick; crossings take either 12.5 hours (direct) or 14.5 hours (with a call at Kirkwall on Orkney), depending on the day. Although the crossing is long and can sometimes be rough in the winter months, the boats are very comfortable with good facilities. Alternatively, the main airport for the islands is at Sumburgh at the southern end, which has daily flights to Inverness (via Orkney), Aberdeen, Glasgow and Edinburgh and also twice weekly to Bergen in Norway.

Once on the islands the road network is very well maintained and away from Lerwick traffic is light. Bus travel requires advance planning, but does reach some surprisingly remote corners. Within Shetland the islands are connected by ferries run by the island's council. Mainland, Yell, Unst, Fetlar, Bressay and Whalsay are all linked by regular vehicle ferries – with the charge usually made in one direction only. Papa Stour and Out Skerries are further out and day visits are possible only on certain days each week. Reaching Foula and Fair Isle requires more planning – daytrips are only possible by air on certain days each week. These need to be booked well in advance and, like some of the longer ferries, are often cancelled at short notice, depending on the weather.

History and culture

The earliest evidence of human habitation in Shetland dates back to beyond 4000BC and the islands are very rich in prehistoric sites. The Norse – previously raiders – began colonising the islands from the 9th century and their culture soon came to dominate. The West Nordic language, Norn, was still spoken here up until the 19th century.

Orkney and Shetland became a Norse Earldom, but in the following centuries Scotland grew increasingly interested in the islands. Ongoing hostilities culminated in the Battle of Largs in 1263 in Ayrshire, with the eventual outcome that Scotland took control of the Hebrides, though Orkney and Shetland remained Norse at first. By the 15th century, Denmark controlled Norway and King Christian I ceded both Orkney and Shetland to the Scots as a marriage dowry – with the condition that they could be bought back by his heirs. The islands became a part of the Scottish Kingdom and all subsequent attempts by the Danes to redeem them were ignored.

Regardless, the connection with Norway has remained strong. When Norway became an independent country again in 1906, Shetlanders sent a letter to the King stating: 'Today no foreign flag is more familiar or more welcome in our voes and havens than that of Norway, and Shetlanders continue to look upon Norway as their motherland, and recall with pride and affection the time when their forefathers were under the rule of the kings of Norway'.

Perhaps the best known celebration of this Norse heritage today is in the Up Helly Aa fire festivals. These are held throughout Shetland in January, with the largest and best known in Lerwick. The ceremonies only actually date back to the late 19th century, but have now grown to be the islands' major cultural event. A different man each year is chosen to be the 'Jarl', and his squad of followers is elaborately dressed as Vikings. Other squads wear a variety of different costumes, and all take part in a torchlit procession which culminates in the torches being thrown to set alight a replica Viking longship. Afterwards each of the local halls are visited, where all-night parties are held, with each squad performing an act – a dance or song which is usually a humorous take on local events or current affairs – and then taking a turn on the floor with the female audience members, making the ceilidh band earn its crust as they are kept playing till dawn.

Fishing has long been central to the islands' economy and remains important today, with further employment in agriculture, renewable energy and tourism. But it was the discovery of North Sea oil in the 1970s that enabled Shetland to avoid the economic decline that has affected some other remote communities. The massive oil terminal at Sullom Voe is the largest in Europe and taxes from the oil revenues have been paid into a charitable trust to help fund local public services.

Accommodation
Outside Lerwick accommodation is fairly scarce, but there is a range of bed and breakfasts, hotels and self-catering cottages, as well as several hostels and campsites. There is also an expanding network of stopovers with facilities for campervans. Peculiar to Shetland are camping böds which offer low-cost and very basic self-catering accommodation, usually in restored historic buildings – the name böd meaning a building used to house fishermen and their gear.

Unst is the most northerly inhabited island in the British archipelago and the last outpost before the ocean stretches away towards the Arctic. The famed cliffs and spectacular seabird colonies of Hermaness are a major draw, but there's a second National Nature Reserve here too – the Keen of Hamar, designated for its remarkable plant life. Unst has great variety, from superb sandy beaches such as at Sandwick to dramatic cliffs like those at the Horns of Hagmark – a name which is an unmistakable reminder of the island's rich Norse heritage.

At first glance Yell may seem to be simply a stepping stone on the journey to the far north, with the bleak moorland seen from the main road between the two ferries appearing to offer little to tempt a stop. Those who turn aside and begin to properly explore the island will find Yell is easily the equal of Unst for fine walks. There are some magnificent beaches and wild coastline, and Yell is reputedly the best place in all Shetland to watch otters.

Fetlar is smaller and much less visited, but well repays the effort of those who take the time to reach it. Beyond the Funzie RSPB reserve – famed in birdwatching circles for its rare phalaropes – the eastern coastline has rugged cliffs and huge natural arches.

6

Heading towards the Stuis of Graveland ▶

Unst, Yell and Fetlar

Framgord and Sandwick

Distance 7.5km Time 3 hours
Terrain beach, straightforward coastal
walking with stiles and gates
Map OS Explorer 470 Access no public
transport to the start

**Explore the Viking remains of Framgord
set close to the coastline beyond the
beautiful sands of Sandwick beach.**

This out and back walk starts at
Hannigarth, where there is a car park and
information board, reached by taking a
minor road off the Uyeasound to Muness
road. Begin by climbing a stile and heading
along the track towards the house. Well
before the house turn right over another
stile and follow the grassy path straight
down to a signpost in front of the brilliant
white sands. Turn left here to head around
the back of the bay. Soon the upright
stones of an Iron Age house can be seen
by the shoreline. Archaeologists have
uncovered two Pictish burial sites in the
sand nearby; one contained a polished
stone disc beside the head and the other
was inside a cairn of quartz pebbles.

Keep walking to soon reach an
information board alongside the remains
of a Norse longhouse. Whilst this was
once much further from the sea, the
encroaching waves and sand have taken
their toll, but you can still make out the
shape of the building and the distinctive
opening to the byre at the north end
which is wider at the top to ease the
passage of a cow.

Either keep going on the grass or drop onto the beach, heading for a stile at the far end of the sands. Once over the stile, keep north and soon the stone walls of the cemetery come into view. Aim towards this – the access gate is round the far side. Within the cemetery are the remains of a Viking chapel, thought to have been associated with the farmstead of Framgord – the remains of an outbuilding dating from the same period have been discovered just outside the cemetery. Take time to explore the graveyard as there are also some very rare Viking keelstones, or burial markers – one decorated with a sword – and also some small Viking crosses. The burial ground is still in use; coffins are often brought across the moor by tractor whilst the mourners make the journey on foot.

Continue the walk by going down towards the shore and turning north, soon reaching a stile in a stone wall. Look out for the shallow dips at the water's edge. These are the remains of noosts – protective shelters for boats hauled out from the water. Noosts are still in use in parts of Shetland, but the ones here are thought to date back to Viking times and

were probably used by the original inhabitants of Framgord farm themselves. Stay close to the shore, keeping a sharp eye out for seals – or the occasional otter.

A fence is crossed at a stile and the ruins of the settlement of Colvadale can be seen on the horizon. The now ruined houses were abandoned at the time of the Highland Clearances. Once you reach the distinctive black shoreline rocks known as the Whale Back you can either head inland to explore the ruins or return to the start by retracing the outward route.

◀ Approaching Sandwick beach

The Keen of Hamar

**Distance 5.5km Time 2 hours
Terrain pathless coastal walking, some
short steep climbs, unprotected cliff,
stiles, minor road Map OS Explorer 470
Access bus stop at Baltasound (600m from
start) – connects to ferry and Lerwick**

**The Keen of Hamar's geology has led
to its unique flora and status as a
National Nature Reserve. Explore this
rare habitat before climbing to the top
of spectacular cliffs, returning alongside
Balta Sound.**

The car park for the Keen of Hamar is at
Littlehamar, a short way from Baltasound
and an easy walk from Unst's furnished
bus stop which has become one of the
island's best known attractions. If driving,
follow the signs for the Keen of Hamar and
turn off the A968 at the bus stop to reach
the car park a short distance further on.
There are usually leaflets available here
and it's worth picking one up to help you
identify any flowers. Start the walk

through the pedestrian gate, keeping the
fence on your right. This fenced corridor
is used to move cattle across the fragile
environment of the Keen of Hamar. Go
through a gate and then over the two stiles
on the right to enter the reserve itself.

This area is renowned to botanists and
geologists alike because it is so rare to find
underlying serpentine rock on the earth's
surface. The serpentine was formed deep
beneath the sea and pushed up by huge
movements of the earth around 400
million years ago. Although it appears
barren – almost lunar – at first glance, the
rock has actually weathered over time to
form a thin soil and if you peer closely
many tiny flowering plants can be spotted.
One of the easier ones to pick out is the
white-flowered Edmonston's chickweed,
known locally as Shetland mouse ear
which only grows here on Unst. It was
discovered by local lad Thomas
Edmonston, who developed a profound
interest in plants from an early age.

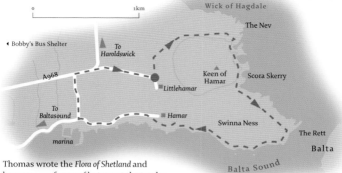

Wick of Hagdale

The Nev

◀ Bobby's Bus Shelter

To
Haroldswick

A968

Keen of
Hamar

Scora Skerry

Littlehamar

To
Baltasound

Hamar

Swinna Ness

The Rett

marina

Balta

Balta Sound

0   1km

Thomas wrote the *Flora of Shetland* and became a professor of botany at the tender age of 20 before losing his life on a scientific expedition to South America just a few months later.

Aim northeast (diagonally left as you face uphill away from the stile) to traverse the rough slopes, aiming towards the sea. Before you come to a fence, turn right to head more directly east towards the sea cliffs. Before reaching the edge, bear right and climb the steep ground above the cliffs. Directly below, the sea surges against the rocks and there are impressive views across to the Hill of Clibberswick to the north (visited on the Horns of Hagmark walk). After some time, you meet a fence and a stile with a view ahead down the hill to Swinna Ness and the island of Balta beyond. Keep following the coastline until another fence forces you inland for a short distance. At a fence junction, cross the fence ahead and then go over the stile on the left to continue downhill, keeping close to the coastline and aiming for the headland of Swinna Ness to soon pick up a better path.

Round the headland to the right and continue west alongside Balta Sound, eventually crossing another stile. Stay near the shore and, at the stone wall, aim for the farm gate between two stiles, going through this to pass below the house with the fence on your right. Continue to make for the white bungalow to shortly join the road; turn left along it towards Baltasound.

Follow the road as it turns right alongside an industrial building to finally reach a memorial to Swedish fishermen who erected a fisher-church in Baltasound in 1910. Turn right here, following a road which leads past the hotel before turning right again at the main road towards Bobby's Shelter. The shelter is named after a seven-year-old local boy who prevented its removal after writing to the council explaining that it was needed as he stored his bike in it whilst at school. The bus shelter has been decorated and furnished by locals for several years, with a regularly changing theme. From here it is only a short walk up the Keen of Hamar approach road to return to the car park.

The Horns of Hagmark

Distance 9km **Time** 3 hours 30
Terrain straightforward clifftop, minor
roads **Map** OS Explorer 470
Access bus to Saxa Vord, Haroldswick –
connects to ferry and Lerwick

Climb to the summit of the Hill of
Clibberswick, perched high above
vertiginous cliffs, feasting your eyes on
some of Unst's finest coastal features,
including the Horns of Hagmark, before
returning inland to visit the former RAF
base of Saxa Vord, where there is an
exhibition and café.

The route starts from the former Saxa
Vord RAF base which now houses holiday
accommodation, a café, an exhibition and
a distillery – it is labelled as 'Valsgarth' on
many OS maps and located just north of
Haroldswick. There is a car park on the
edge of the Saxa Vord complex.

Begin the walk by heading east along
the minor road towards Skeggie, where
you turn right. Ignore the turn to
Gerratown but take the next left signed
for Clibberswick. At the end of the public
road keep left to pass around the back of
the quarry (Britain's only working talc
quarry) and then aim towards the coast
to pick up a faint grassy path along the
clifftop. Talc is formed from serpentine,
the rare rock that makes up the Keen of
Hamar reserve, which can be seen across
the bay. There is also evidence near here
of Norse quarrying of soapstone, which is
formed from talc, and which was used by

the Vikings for bowls, cooking plates and other utensils.

Keep following the coastline, climbing a stile by a ruin and then another stile as the going becomes rougher. Stay to the left of a walled enclosure and divert slightly inland to pass a deep geo. Soon the first dramatic view of the great cliffs appears – a wall of rock plunging 160m from the highest point to the sea below. The views just keep on improving as the walk climbs steeply to reach the trig point at the Hill of Clibberswick's summit, with its 360-degree panorama of island and sea.

Hug the clifftop, veering to the right at one point to aim for a stile over a fence. Beyond these are the Horns of Hagmark – several large rocks which project clear of the horizon, making a memorable landmark when seen from the sea. The coastal features continue as the route descends, particularly looking down on the promontory above Ship Stack. Above Girr Wick a number of old enclosures known as kailyards – once used to grow kail and other animal fodder – are passed. The sandy beach of Nor Wick stretches out

below. As the route approaches the beach, angle left up the field towards the houses at Millfield and go through a gate to reach the track. Follow this behind the houses; it soon becomes a minor road.

At Kirkaton turn left and left again at the next junction to return towards Saxa Vord. The RAF has operated a radar station here since World War II. Its effect on Unst has been dramatic, bringing electricity to the island in the mid-1950s, jobs and a mini-population boom. Since 2007 much of the site has been redeveloped as a tourism enterprise with the radar equipment on neighbouring Saxa Vord hill being serviced by only a small number of resident staff, although the base station is currently in the process of reactivation.

◂ Cliffs below the Hill of Clibberswick

13

Hermaness

Distance 10.5km **Time** 3 hours 30
Terrain clear, waymarked path to cliff,
some steep boggy ground
Map OS Explorer 470 **Access** no public
transport to the start

**Explore Shetland's greatest seabird city
with more than 100,000 nesting birds on
the dramatic cliffs, and views out to
Muckle Flugga and beyond.**

The Hermaness car park is at the end of
a narrow road from Haroldswick; take the
signed left fork at the end. If time allows
you may want to check out the visitor
centre, found by walking down the right-
hand fork in the road and housed in an old
lighthouse shore station.

Start the walk by heading through the
gate and climbing the excellent path across
the open moor. Looking right there are
views to the RAF station on the summit of
Saxa Vord across the Burra Firth. After a

short distance the path becomes a
boardwalk, keeping walkers off the boggy
ground; follow it, aiming gently uphill
along the north side of the Burn of
Winnaswarta Dale. In summer you will see
great skuas, or bonxies as they are locally
known. These huge ground-nesting birds
are sometimes called the 'pirates of the sky'
for their habit of harassing other birds into
regurgitating or dropping their own catch.
They will also ruthlessly defend their
territory when breeding, so with about 750
pairs here it's wise not to get too close.

The landscape changes utterly as you
reach the top of the massive cliff walls.
Take care near the edge: it's a 140m drop to
the ocean below and the short and uneven
turf can be slippery. Depending on whether
you are primarily a puffin or a gannet fan
there is a choice of route. To visit the huge
gannetry of the Neap turn left to bear
south along the clifftop. As you climb, the

◄ Gannets on a sea stack off Hermaness

smell from the 30,000 pairs of gannets is the first sign that you will soon be staring into a flying cloud of these elegant dive-bombing fishing experts.

The best views of the gannets come as the route continues around the cliffs, descending a little and keeping close to the coast to reach Saito. Here you can look back on the white cliffs of the Neap. Other parts of the cliffs at Hermaness are home to 15 species of seabird, including guillemots, razorbills, fulmars, kittiwakes and shags. However, if puffins are your bag return past the Neap to where the path first reached the cliffs.

Most of the puffin colonies are found to the north from here, usually in burrows excavated by themselves or in old rabbit burrows in the soil near the top of the cliffs. About five percent of the UK's population of puffins call Hermaness home, around 25,000 breeding pairs. However, even with this number it is possible to come here and only spot a handful of these colourful and characterful birds. They arrive from mid-April and leave in early August, but for the first weeks of the breeding season will often be out at sea during the day, so the best time is likely to be late afternoon or early evening as they come back from their fishing trips.

Later in the season, with hungry chicks to look after, one of each pair will be on guard duty while the other fishes so the ground is often teeming.

Keep following the coast, descending steeply after Toolie and passing more gannet colonies on large sea stacks. There are good views to Muckle Flugga and its lighthouse and Out Stack. The going becomes rougher and wet underfoot, and eventually the 'path' swings right uphill. From here turn back and retrace the outward route to the start.

Map labels:

Looss Wick

The Gord

Taing of Loosswick

The Framd

The Greing

Humla Stack

Clingra Stack

Hermaness Hill

Wurs Stack

Flodda Stack

Brim Ness

Sothers Stack

Hermaness National Nature Reserve

Shorda Hellier

Kame of Flouravoug

Toolie

Neap

Burn of Winnaswarta Dale

Burra Firth

Saito

Mouslee Hill

Fiska Wick

0   1km

visitor centre

B9086

To Haroldswick

Root Stacks

Heoga Ness and Ladies Hole

Distance 5.25km **Time** 2 hours
Terrain clear coastal walking, some
pathless sections **Map** OS Explorer 470
Access nearest bus stop at Burravoe
School, 1km from the start; connects to
ferries and Lerwick

**Round the coastal headland of Heoga
Ness before heading for a semi-circular
inlet backed by high cliffs and popular
with nesting puffins and other seabirds.**

Begin from Burravoe's pier and marina
where there is parking, a small campsite
and toilets. Note the roof of the toilet block
which is made from an upturned lifeboat
originally from the cruise ship *Canberra*. Go
through the gate on the left as you face the
water and follow the path along the edge
of Burra Voe, 'voe' being the name given to
deep inlets or small fjords in both Orkney
and Shetland. Continue around the head

of the voe, keeping the shore on
your right and passing behind the remains
of a methodist chapel dating from 1827.
The south shore of Burra Voe has a track
to follow and gives good views across to
the marina and to the castellated
merchant's house or haa. A much earlier
merchant's haa built in 1672 is now open
as a fascinating museum and tearoom
in the centre of Burravoe and is well worth
a visit. It also houses a collection of
wildlife photographs by Bobby Tulloch,
a renowned local naturalist and
photographer whose affection for
snowy owls and campaigning for avian
conservation earned him the nickname
'the Birdman of Shetland'.

Keep following the coast to round the
headland of Outer Virdik and continue
along the far side. This is a good area to
look out for seals and otters, or 'dratsies' to

◄ Burra Voe

give them their Shetland name. An old stone circular 'otter house', once used as a trap, can be seen up on the left. When you reach the pebble bank separating the small Loch of Vatswick from the sea, keep on the inland side of the stone causeway and continue following the shore, now aiming for the headland of Cumlins.

After crossing another area of pebbly shingle you arrive at Whal Wick, also a fine place to watch out for otters. Carry on round the small headland and then aim inland along the south side of a deep inlet, the Geo of Gardins, which lies almost opposite Burra Voe. A gap in the stone wall leads to a gate after which you return to the coast and climb the steep ground, heading for the fence protecting the cliff edge. From here you can stare

down over Ladies Hole. The high cliffs here house large colonies of guillemots, cormorants, razorbills and kittiwakes and smaller numbers of puffins which nest in burrows at the top.

The walk can be lengthened by climbing above the cliffs and following the coast towards the impressive Stack of the Horse, a large sea arch with caves nearby. However, this shorter walk heads back downhill across the narrow strip of land to pick up the outward path. From here it retraces the route alongside Burra Voe to the marina and the start.

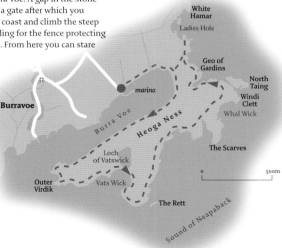

The White Wife of Otterswick

**Distance 6.75km Time 2 hours 30
Terrain signed path, then rough and
boggy coastal walking, stiles, minor road
Map OS Explorer 470 Access bus stop at
Aywick on the route – connects to
ferries and Lerwick**

**The White Wife is a striking shipwreck
memorial set on the coast in an area
known as Otterswick which, as its name
suggests, is one of the best places for
spotting otters in Shetland.**

Start from the minor road junction just
west of East Yell hall – there is usually
space to park here without blocking any
access, or parking may be available near the
hall. Once on foot follow the minor road
towards Queyon which is signed for the
White Wife. Turn right at another sign
where the road becomes a track, keeping to
the right of the fence. After a corner cross
the stile and then head down to the

shoreline, aiming left along it to reach the
wooden figurehead known as the White
Wife. During a storm in 1924 a German
boat, the *Bohus*, was wrecked on the rocks
offshore and rapidly sank. Four of the
39 crew perished, including a young cadet
who saved four of his shipmates' lives
before he himself was drowned. Later that
year the figurehead washed ashore and
was erected by locals as a memorial.
More recently it has been restored and
remains a striking reminder of the
savagery of the sea.

From the White Wife keep following the
coastline along the low cliffs which can be
wet underfoot in places. After a gate pass a
wooden seat and stay on the coast as the
route crosses open ground and heads
around the Ness of Queyon.

Keep to the back of a pebble bay and take
note of the signs when a fence is reached.
The usual way is through the gate to stay

◀ The White Wife shipwreck memorial

on the coastal side of the fence, but if livestock is being grazed on this land the sign will indicate that you should take the alternative route on the left side of the fence using the stile. Either way, keep the coast in view and an eye open for any passing porpoises or otters.

Yell is a particular otter hotspot because of its combination of shallow offshore water providing plentiful food, low peaty coastline which is ideal for digging holts, and abundant freshwater which otters need to clean the saltwater from their pelts. They are often seen in the bay at Aywick: watch out for the distinctive

V-shape in the water as they swim along. Although they are harder to spot on land, they do like to come ashore onto the rocks to eat, groom themselves or sometimes just laze around. They also venture further inland seeking freshwater and holts.

Keep following the shore until a walkers' gate immediately before a burn, go through the gate and turn left up the field with the fence on your right to soon reach a track. Turn right along this to a minor road which leads past the shop at Aywick. At the next junction carry straight on and follow the minor road back to the start.

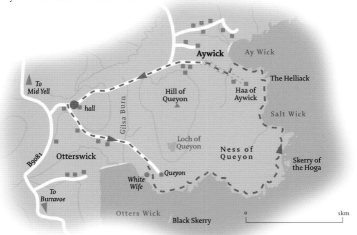

Stuis of Graveland

Distance 11.5km **Time** 5 hours
Terrain rough, pathless moorland,
navigation skills needed, some fences
to cross **Map** OS Explorer 470
Access no public transport to the start

**A tough moorland yomp leads out onto
a wild peninsula known as the Stuis of
Graveland, a beautifully remote and
atmospheric place.**

The walk starts from the approach road
to the farm at Efstigarth – there is usually
space to park without blocking access
about 200m before the farm buildings.
To reach this point turn off the A968 near
Mid Yell, signed for Grimister, and then
fork left for Efstigarth. From here begin by
going over the stile on the far side of the
road and heading uphill, following the line
of a burn and then aiming northwest to
reach a gated junction of four fences to the
west of the farm. Cross the two gates to
reach the moorland on the opposite side
and then continue northwest to climb over
the rough ground.

This soon becomes a broad ridge which
is followed northwards towards the
summit of Virdi Field, crossing another
fenceline along the way. From the summit
the panoramic views show Whale Firth to
the east and a collection of hill lochs
backed by Yell Sound, Fethaland and the
Ramna Stacks to the west. Keep straight on
down to the peaty bealach below Stany
Hill, stepping over another fence at a
support post.

Keep north and soon you come to the highest point of Stany Hill. From here the view is down to the dramatic cliffs above a projecting rock fin known as the Eigg. When you reach the clifftops keep well back as they are unstable and bear right to follow the coast – with much-improved ground underfoot. At a deep inlet – or geo – called Mass John's House, detour slightly to the right to reach a gate in the fence and then continue north along the cliffs of Green Hill. The impressive and unnatural-looking rock fang of Ern Stack pierces the view – looking decidedly precarious.

Here the walking is easier – rabbits have cropped the low grass – as the route descends beyond the Hill of the Standing Stone, aiming for the far tip of the peninsula. An inlet near the end almost makes an island of the Nev of Stuis which overlooks some small sea stacks and is ideal for looking out for passing sea creatures. The very remote and wild coastline of Yell stretches northwards across the other side of Whale Firth.

The easiest return route is to retrace the outward walk, climbing back up along the cliff and enjoying the different coastal views before the moorland trot and descent back down to the road.

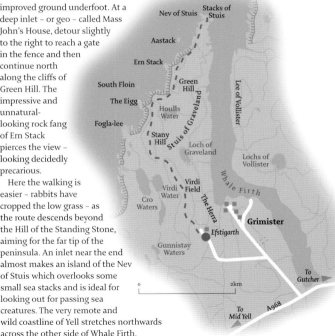

Nev of Stuis
Stacks of Stuis
Aastack
Ern Stack
South Floin
Green Hill
The Eigg
Houlls Water
Fogla-lee
Stany Hill
Stuis of Graveland
Loch of Graveland
Lee of Vollister
Lochs of Vollister
Virdi Field
Virdi Water
Cro Waters
The Herra
Whale Firth
Gunnistay Waters
Efstigarth
Grimister
To Gutcher
To Mid Yell
A968

0   2km

◀ The wild northwest coast of Yell seen from the Stuis of Graveland

21

Sands of Breckon and Gloup Ness

Distance 9km **Time** 4 hours 30
Terrain some pathless rough and boggy
sections, stiles, minor road
Map OS Explorer 470 **Access** no public
transport to the start

**Explore one of the most lovely beaches on
Yell before venturing along the remote
coastline to the former coastguard
lookout at Gloup Ness with its stunning
views to Unst and Muckle Flugga beyond.**

Start from Breckon, where there is a
signed car park. Walk through the gate
onto the track (signed for Breckon Sands).
Soon the spectacular beach comes into
view; however, this route bypasses it at
first, carrying straight on after a stile to
follow a path marked with white stones.
Cross a boardwalk and then climb uphill to
another stile. The grassy path aims north

and then northwest to cross the dunes and
arrive at the shore at the southern end of
the Ness of Houlland. At the coast turn left
to walk alongside a fence above a deep
inlet and then pass through a gate in the
wall. This is the most northerly headland
of Yell; go out onto it until an impassable
geo cuts across, then return along the far
side towards the white Sands of Breckon.

Once over a stile in the wall descend to
reach the beach, which is often empty – if
there is anyone else here then locals would
say it was busy. Walk to the far end of the
beach to climb some wooden steps and
follow a path to the gate. It is possible to
shortcut back to the start from here, but
this route continues along the coast,
staying level with the low cliffs and
becoming much rougher underfoot. Keep
using the stiles to cross the fences,

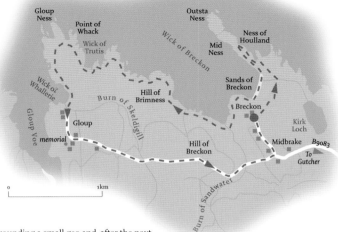

Gloup
Ness
Point of
Whack
Wick of
Trutis
Outsta
Ness
Wick of Breckon
Mid
Ness
Ness of
Houlland
Wick of
Whallerie
Hill of
Brimness
Burn of Skeldgill
Sands of
Breckon
Breckon
Kirk
Loch
Gloup Voe
Gloup
memorial
Hill of
Breckon
Midbrake
B9083
To
Gutcher
Burn of Sandwater

0   1km

rounding a small geo and, after the next bay, pass a ruined watermill once used to mill oats and barley. Wooden boardwalks cover the wettest ground. Keep right at a junction, soon going through a gate and then onto a more open section of coastline with the occasional white marker post indicating the route.

The cliffs have now grown in stature and from the final headland of Gloup Ness the path climbs uphill past a couple of benches, giving great views towards the west coast of Unst and the cliffs of Hermaness, with Muckle Flugga just visible beyond. The highest point of the hill is crowned by the old coastguard lookout, which has been delightfully renovated and furnished by a local crofter whose father was paid to undertake coastguard shifts at this amazing lookout point.

Keep briefly west, following the marker posts, until the route turns south towards the settlement of Gloup. Join a track and pass through the gate to reach the minor road leading to Gloup. It is worth detouring to the right to view the Gloup fishing memorial, a moving tribute to the 58 fishermen who perished in an unexpected summer storm in 1881, leaving 34 widows and 85 fatherless children. The disaster heralded the beginning of the end for the use of Shetland sixareens, open fishing boats propelled by six oars, which would take to sea for two or three days at a time and offered very little protection from the elements. Return to the road and continue along it past the houses of Gloup and the crofting land, turning left after 2.5km to return to the parking area at the start.

◀ Approaching the Sands of Breckon

23

The Snap and the Loch of Funzie

Distance 8.25km Time **3 hours 30**
Terrain **pathless and boggy coast in
places, stiles, minor roads**
Map **OS Explorer 470** Access **Fetlar dial-a-
ride must be booked by 4:30pm the
day before**

**This fantastic circular walk takes in
some of the finest stretches of Fetlar's
coastline, as well as visiting the RSPB
reserve at the Loch of Funzie.**

Fetlar attracts birdwatchers from around
the country keen to spot one of Britain's
rarest breeding birds, the red-necked
phalarope, but it is well worth taking the
time to explore some of its dramatic and
wild coastline, too. This route starts from
the Loch of Funzie (pronounced 'finnie')
car park on the B9088. A feature wall has

been built here from local rocks to
illustrate the stretching and squashing of
these rare conglomerates over the passage
of millions of years. Start by turning right
out of the car park to head east along the
road, soon passing the loch. The red-
necked phalaropes usually arrive in late
May, staying until the end of July to raise
their young. The loch has around half the
UK's breeding population and these small
wading birds are relatively easy to spot,
with the female being the larger and more
colourful of the pair and the male taking
on all the incubating and chick-rearing
jobs. Whimbrels, which are similar to the
larger curlew, are also a Fetlar speciality,
but sadly snowy owls – which bred here
back in the 1960s and '70s – have not been
sighted since 1995. A bird hide overlooking

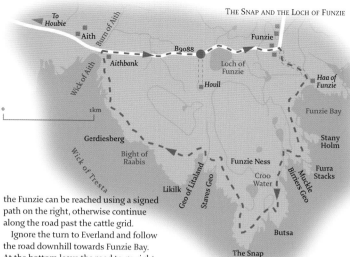

the Funzie can be reached using a signed path on the right, otherwise continue along the road past the cattle grid.

Ignore the turn to Everland and follow the road downhill towards Funzie Bay. At the bottom leave the road to go right, taking a faint path on the left side of a burn flowing directly towards the sea. By the bay turn right over a footbridge (signed for Snap Walk), soon crossing a stile and continuing along the wall towards the house. Pass through a gate and keep left of the house, picking up a clifftop path that climbs steeply and gives great views. Go over the stone wall by a stile, then keep on the right side of the fence until another stile; once over this stay on a small clifftop path traversing the slope.

After a gate in a fence pass the Furra Stacks and then a couple of deep inlets, or geos, before the headland of Butsa. Stay close to the cliff to view a massive natural arch en route to the headland known as The Snap. A vague path following the coastline can be picked up after rounding

the headland. This is a good area to spot Arctic terns, which nest nearby. After a fenced geo aim for the back of another deep inlet and climb the stile. The ground behind the Geo of Litaland can be very wet underfoot so choose the easiest route to continue round the coast, where eider ducks are often seen. There is another stile before the houses of Aith eventually come into view. Follow a stone wall on the seaward side, climb two stiles and bear left for the bottom of the garden at Aithbank, then pass in front of its garden to reach the road. This house is now a camping böd providing basic accommodation to visitors. Turn right along the road to return to the start, noting the row of stone circular shelters known as planticrubs which were used to grow kail and other crops.

◀ Natural arch on the way to The Snap

Strandburgh Ness

Distance 9.5km **Time** 3 hours 30
Terrain pathless clifftop, rough and
exposed in places, stiles, minor roads
Map OS Explorer 470 **Access** Fetlar dial-a-
ride must be booked by 4:30pm the
day before

**Discover some of Fetlar's wild coastline,
including the site of an old fishing station
and a monastic community, before
returning through fertile croftland that
illustrates why the island is known as
'The Garden of Shetland'.**

Begin from Everland, reached by turning
north from the B9088 after the Loch of
Funzie. Ensure no gates are blocked when
parking and start the walk by passing to
the left of the farmhouse, heading between
it and a metal shed and climbing a stile.
Now aim diagonally towards the sea to
reach the ruins of Smithfield Haa, a large
merchant's house built in 1815 but
abandoned by 1870. Keep to the left of the
ruin and once over a stile head diagonally

downhill across the field to another
stile over a stone wall. Beyond this keep
level with the shore and after one more
stile the route continues along the now
unfenced coastline.

Follow the coast out to the small
headland of Hesta Ness, crossing a stile
in a derelict wall and then a burn where
the ruins of a Norse mill can still be seen.
These small water-powered grain mills
were used for oats and barley and are a
feature of many watercourses in Shetland.
You can still see the route the water
would have taken through the tiny
building to power the grinding stones.
Fetlar is said to have been the first place
the Vikings landed when they journeyed
west to Shetland.

After Hesta Ness you pass a long inlet
called Skarpi Geo. From the back of this
geo climb to a stile in a stone wall and
cross the sometimes wet ground at Longa
Tonga, where the remains of early 20th-
century winding gear can still be seen,

◄ Ruin of Smithfield Haa

originally used when soapstone was quarried from the cliffs. As the route nears its objective of Strandburgh Ness the cliffs become more dramatic and a series of deep inlets bite into the coast.

Strandburgh Ness is made up of Outer Brough – an island cut off by a narrow channel of swirling water – and Inner Brough, which is itself isolated from the rest of Fetlar by a narrow neck of land. Such a position made it attractive to those seeking solitude and it once housed a Norse monastic clifftop community. To reach it you have to pass through the site of more Viking buildings, the ruins visible on the narrow land bridge as you head out onto Inner Brough. From the far edge you can look across the channel to Outer Brough, which also has Norse remains.

Return across the neck of land from Inner Brough and then keep going south along the coastline, enjoying a succession of impressive rock features, including fine caves. There is a good natural arch which is best seen by detouring onto the Head of Cumla and looking back. The Birdens is a collection of small sea stacks; beyond these aim left to reach a stile in a fence and then make for the back of Whale Geo. The

going gets tougher as the route rises to keep above the cliffs. After another stile go right to cross a bridge over a burn and then stay near the coast before eventually walking inland behind Houlls Geo. Cross a stile near a gate and then follow a boardwalk before dropping directly down towards Funzie Bay. The house on your left, Haa of Funzie, was formerly a fishing station and there is an information board nearby. Turn right at the road to climb the hill and then right near the top to return to Everland.

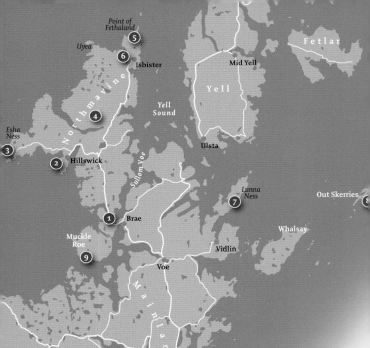

Northmavine is the northernmost part of Shetland's Mainland, joined to the rest of the island by the narrow isthmus of Mavis Grind. This is the wildest part of the main island and also has the highest hills in Shetland. The spectacular cliff scenery around Esha Ness makes it a must-visit, whilst lonely Fethaland and

Uyea offer walks that will live long in the memory. Inland, Ronas Hill rises above all, a vast sweep of tundra reminiscent of the Arctic.

Across Mavis Grind, Northmavine houses the massive Sullom Voe oil terminal, but it is tucked away and the wide landscapes elsewhere are well worth exploring. This area is also the gateway to several islands. Muckle Roe offers one of Shetland's finest and most rugged walks, whilst remote Out Skerries make an essential destination for island baggers.

North Mainland, Muckle Roe and Skerries

Mavis Grind and the Islesburgh tomb

Distance 2.25km **Time** 1 hour
Terrain tracks, pathless steep grass,
stiles **Map** OS Explorer 470
Access bus from Lerwick

Mavis Grind may sound like a 1940s
dance number but is, in fact, a narrow
isthmus of land connecting Northmavine
to the rest of Shetland Mainland, so
slender that it is said to be possible to toss
a stone from the North Sea and have it
land in the Atlantic. This short ramble
climbs above the Grind and then descends
to visit a well-preserved prehistoric
chambered cairn.

There is a large lay-by on the west side
of the A970 just to the south of Mavis
Grind. From here walk north along the
verge and through a gate where there are
information boards.

The narrows of Mavis Grind were long
used as a portage point where boats
would be carried for the short overland trip
to avoid the long and treacherous sea
journey around the northern end of
Mainland. In 1999 Shetlanders employed
their muscle power to demonstrate that
Vikings could have used this route more
than 1000 years ago, by pulling an eight-
tonne replica Viking trading ship over the
Grind, although the sheer effort involved
convinced many archaeologists that boats

of that size would probably have remained in the water.

Another gate leads onto grassy land and a large fenced picnic area. Go straight across this and through a gate on the far side, turn left and climb up the track to a quarry. Ignore the first entrance to the quarry and stay on the track until the next entrance. Leave the track here and bear left over grass and then steeply downhill (with care) aiming for a turning area on the track down by the shore below.

When you reach this track turn right along it. Climb a stile to leave the track when it heads inland, instead continuing around the back of the bay. A further stile leads to a faint path which keeps to the

shoreline and then a gate and a section of fenced path, before the route crosses rougher ground to reach the chambered cairn ahead.

This Neolithic structure is a good example of a heel-shaped burial tomb. Although it was excavated in 1959 nothing was found inside at that time. There are also circular and D-shaped prehistoric enclosures nearby. Return by the same outward route from which there's a great view over Mavis Grind as the quarry track descends.

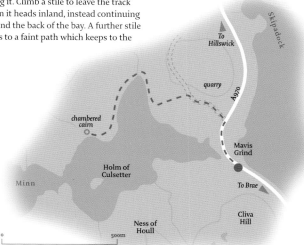

◀ Looking back from the chambered cairn

Ness of Hillswick

Distance 7.75km **Time** 3 hours 30
Terrain pathless grassy clifftops, stiles
Map OS Explorer 470
Access bus from Lerwick

This delightful coastal exploration of the Ness of Hillswick peninsula takes in some spectacular cliff scenery, including the Drongs sea stacks, and a visit to a tiny lighthouse at the furthest point.

The walk starts from the shoreside parking area near the public toilets in Hillswick. To reach it turn left opposite the imposing St Magnus Bay Hotel and head down past the shop. Well before Nordic flatpacks became household favourites, the hotel was manufactured in Norway more than 100 years ago and erected at Kelvingrove in Glasgow for an exhibition before being moved to its current location.

Start by walking southwest along the lane between the toilets and the large house – home of the Hillswick Wildlife Sanctuary which cares for sick or abandoned seal and otter pups. Continue along the road as it bears left and keep following it until it bends right at the far end of the bay. Turn left here to climb a stile and take the rough track towards the sea. Another stile leads to the grassy coastline; keep aiming right to follow the coast, with an eye open for swimming otters. After passing a flattish bay a gate leads towards Tur Ness and the cliffs begin to grow in stature, with a couple of sea arches below.

After a further stile a path leads towards a sheep enclosure. Keep to the right of this, climbing another stile to pass around the back of a low-lying bay known as the

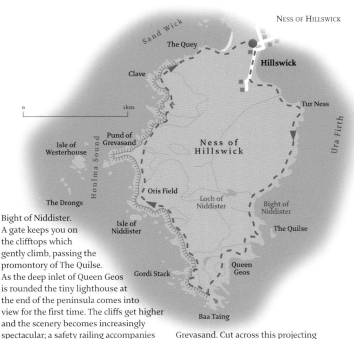

Bight of Niddister.
A gate keeps you on the clifftops which gently climb, passing the promontory of The Quilse. As the deep inlet of Queen Geos is rounded the tiny lighthouse at the end of the peninsula comes into view for the first time. The cliffs get higher and the scenery becomes increasingly spectacular; a safety railing accompanies the final stretch to the lighthouse.

The return from the lighthouse is along the western side of the Ness and has the best views. The impressive Gordi Stack is suddenly revealed, changing shape from a needle to a fin as you follow the cliffs and view it from different angles. Further out to sea are the Drongs, a series of dramatic granite pinnacles which were climbed by famed mountaineers Mick Fowler, Andy Nisbet, John Lincoln and Craig Jones in 1992.

Go over Oris Field to reveal great views of the cliffs curving round to the Pund of Grevasand. Cut across this projecting peninsula and regain the cliffs shortly beyond it. Pass through a gate and round the end of a deep geo before climbing steeply to the right beside a fence and aiming directly for the next grassy hilltop shown as point 82m on OS maps – another fine viewpoint.

Return to the clifftop and descend, heading through a gate to reach the beautiful bay at Sand Wick. To return to the start of the walk, keep left of a wall and fence and then aim right across a grassy pasture before crossing a stile and turning left on the road.

◀ Sea stack off the Ness of Hillswick

33

Esha Ness and Tangwick

Distance 13.75km Time 5 hours
Terrain grassy clifftop, rough in places,
stiles, minor roads Map OS Explorer 469
Access no public transport to the start

**Explore the high cliffs of the Esha Ness
peninsula on this satisfying circular walk
with plenty of opportunities for seabird
and wildlife spotting. The fascinating
Tangwick Haa Museum, which also serves
refreshments, is a little over halfway.**

Start from the car park at the end of the
road at Eshaness Lighthouse – one of
Shetland's more remote places yet popular
with visitors. Begin by heading to the very
high and sheer cliffs and carefully follow
these to the right, passing right around the
impressively deep inlet of Calder's Geo,
home to many seabirds, including puffins,

during the breeding season. Once on the
far side of the geo stay with the clifftops to
continue north along a coastline featuring
an array of stacks, arches, caves and geos.

Keep left of the Lochs of Dridgeo and
cross a stile over a dyke. The yawning sea
cave at the base of Moo Stack can be seen
from here, as well as an arch further to the
right. Keep following the coast, climbing
stiles over fences as necessary. The cliffs
become lower on the northern side of the
peninsula. Aim for a gap in a drystane dyke
and continue on a grassy path along the
coast. Cross the shingle that divides Croo
Loch from the sea and keep ahead on a
clear path running above the cliffs that rise
around the northern side of the Hill of Ure.
Muckle Ossa – with its own sea arch – can
be seen in the distance. Make your way

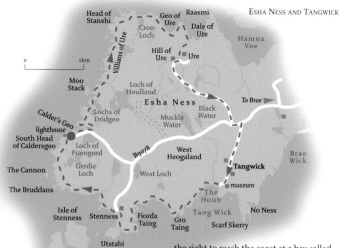

around the back of the Geo of Ure and through a walkers' gate before descending to a couple of stiles. After the next headland aim towards the Dale of Ure but don't go down to the bay; instead turn southwest along a fence until a stile and then a gate leads to the tarmac road end near the house at Ure. Turn left along the road and then right at a junction with a house. Follow this quiet minor road for 1.7km across the moorland interior. At the Esha Ness road turn left for a short distance before turning right, signed for Tangwick. The granite, finger-like pinnacles of the Drongs are seen ahead.

The imposing 17th-century house is Tangwick Haa, once the residence of the local laird and now an interesting museum with a small café. Continue on the track on the right to reach the coast at a bay called the Houb, the Shetland word for a lagoon. Follow the coast, passing a ruin and going through a walkers' gate. This is a good area to see seals and, further on, to enjoy views of Dore Holm with its massive arch. Pass several rocky bays, some with small arches of their own. After another stone ruin keep near the coast, crossing gates and stiles as necessary. Near Stenness the route climbs between two fences and crosses more stiles to reach a memorial cross high above the sea. From here descend to another stile and round the Fiorda Taing, eventually crossing the pebble beach below Stenness. Keep left of the ruined building and from the bay bear left to reach a stile on grassy slopes above the coastline. After a ruin, a stile and a larger stile over a wall, pass above The Bruddans and The Cannon as the ground climbs towards the high cliffs of Eshaness Lighthouse.

◀ Stack off Esha Ness

Ronas Hill

Distance 6.5km **Time** 4 hours
Terrain pathless stony ground, some
boggy areas, navigation skills needed
Map OS Explorer 470 **Access** no public
transport to the start

**Climb to the highest summit in Shetland,
the wild and windswept Arctic tundra of
Ronas Hill. The views are superb, but the
landscape is bleak, pathless and very
exposed – definitely one to blow the
cobwebs away.**

It is usually possible to drive up to a
parking area at the telecommunications
masts on the summit of Collafirth Hill; the
service road is unmarked and potholed
initially, but improves higher up, although
care is still needed. It is accessed from the
A970 just beyond North Collafirth.

Although this makes for a relatively high
starting point, the route from here is
pathless and the rocky terrain devoid of
any landmarks, so a map and compass
(and navigation skills) are essential.
Poor weather and low visibility are
common here.

Begin by descending slightly to Uyea
Scord; this first part is actually the
roughest underfoot of the whole route.
The terrain bears more resemblance to
Arctic tundra than the normal Shetland
vegetation. After the low point the route
climbs to a cairn; from here the going
becomes much better as the route rises up
to Roga Field, which is also marked with a
prominent cairn. The walk levels off for a
while before climbing to the wide, open
summit of Mid Field. Descend slightly

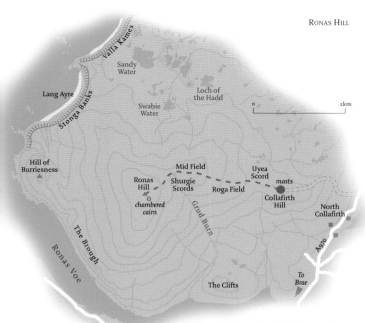

from here to pass just north of the lochan at the bealach of Shurgie Scords.

Now the final dome of Ronas Hill itself must be tackled; a straightforward slog uphill to the stone trig point is rewarded with fabulous views. The wild moorland interior of Northmavine stretches out to the north with the tidal island of Uyea visible in the far distance. As the summit is relatively flat it is necessary to wander around a little to get the best views in all directions; bear briefly southwest to bring the Eshaness peninsula into view. An ancient chambered cairn is set just a short

distance to the southeast of the summit. As a scheduled ancient monument it is protected by law, so do not add to the cairn atop the Neolithic original. Retrace your steps to Collafirth Hill to complete the walk.

Ronas Hill is sometimes crossed en route to the Lang Ayre, thought to be the UK's remotest large beach, situated on the coast to the northwest. Visiting the Lang Ayre is a serious undertaking – a long and very exposed full-day route with an extremely steep descent to reach the southern end of the beach. Tired walkers are then faced with the climb back up and over Ronas Hill for the return.

◀ Summit of Ronas Hill

Fethaland

Distance 10km **Time** 3 hours 30
Terrain rough moorland and grassy
clifftop, tracks, paths, stiles
Map OS Explorer 470 **Access** bus from Brae
to North Roe, 1.2km from the start

**A classic walk to the northernmost point
of Mainland Shetland, this route follows
the rough coastline to visit the
atmospheric ruins of an old fishing
station amidst dramatic scenery.**

There is limited parking near the end of
the public road at Isbister – take care not
to block any entrances or the turning
area. Start by branching right past the
metal barn up a track, passing to the right
of the cemetery. The track is indistinct in
places as it passes to the right of a stone
house and then bends right, going
through a gate with a stile next to it.
Cross the field to a stile over the next
fence, soon reaching some ruins to the
north of the Loch of Houllsquey. Aim for

another stile leading out onto open
ground above the east coast of the
peninsula. The route now continues
northwards over the grazing land above
the cliffs, soon passing the inaccessible
headland of the Kame of Isbister, once the
site of a monastic settlement.

Keep heading north, passing through a
walkers' gate and then descending to a
ruined enclosure at Little Burn. Continue
ahead, climbing to go through another
gate and nearing the coast again as it
traverses the flank of Ramna Beorgs. Carry
on down to a further gate and across a
boggy dip; keep just left of Eislin Geo to
the next gate. As you climb over the
eastern slopes of Skinis Field, stunning
views of the Fethaland peninsula and the
islands beyond open up. Continue just
above Wick of Breibister bay, passing
through gates in a couple more fences as
the going becomes easier underfoot.
A track crosses the narrow strip of land to
the area known as the Isle of Fethaland,

passing the ruins of an Iron Age broch.

Whilst people have lived here since prehistoric times, most of the ruins visible now date from its use as a thriving fishing station from the 15th to the early 20th century. At its busiest up to 60 open row boats known as sixareens would have operated from the station. With six oars each, these were used for multi-day fishing expeditions to points between here and the edge of the continental shelf, an area known as the 'haaf', 80km to the west. The fish were cured and dried on the beach, and the ruins of many of the 36 lodges that would have housed the workers still remain today.

After exploring the ruins continue northwards up to the small modern lighthouse on the Isle of Fethaland, and just beyond. This is the most northerly spot on Mainland Shetland and boasts great views of the Isle of Gruney and the Ramna Stacks, home to a large colony of seabirds. To the southwest the coastline stretches out to the tidal island of Uyea, which can be seen in the distance. Return to Fethaland, crossing the isthmus, and stay on the grassy track as it leads southwest. Soon the track becomes clearer and climbs the hill past the last lodges. Before the track reaches the Upper Loch of Setter turn right and, after 450m, leave the track where it bends right to follow marker posts through a field and over a small footbridge. Continue to a gate and follow the markers as the path runs south,

keeping close to the eastern shores of the Lower Loch of Setter.

When another track is joined follow it south over a low rise, leaving it when it too curves right towards Sandvoe. Instead keep straight on towards some ruined buildings. After these, aim southeast to a walkers' gate in the fence. Cross the next field to return to Isbister, meeting a track at another gate – the start of the walk is just to the right.

Uyea circuit from Sandvoe

Distance 15.5km **Time** 5 hours 30
Terrain rough pathless coast, stony track
for return, navigation skills needed for
outward route **Map** OS Explorer 469
Access bus from Brae to North Roe

**The remote tidal island of Uyea is a truly
magical place, surrounded by sea stacks
and skerries and the views make a
fabulous reward for the tough coastal
walk to get there. The long return is easier
going on a track passing lochans known
for their red-throated divers.**

At Sandvoe there is usually parking near
the cemetery. From here walk towards the
buildings and take the signed gate on the
right. Cross the field, go through another
gate and keep following the coastline on
the west side of Sand Voe, soon aiming
slightly inland to cross a stile and avoid
the very steep ground near the cliffs.

Descend steeply over rough ground to
reach the back of the beach at Roer Mill.
Cross the burn and climb up next to the
ruined fishing böd on the far side of the
beach. Here fishermen in open row boats –
known as sixareens and unique to
Shetland – would dry their catch on the
stones of this sheltered inlet. More
memories, photos and examples of
sixareens can be seen in the excellent
Shetland Museum in Lerwick.

Head diagonally uphill from the ruined
böd and, once up the steep ground, follow
the coast above the high cliffs and around
the headland of Heoga Neap. Look ahead
as you go around the deep inlet of Raa
Wick to choose your route over the bumpy
terrain – generally the easier ground is
found by descending to stay as close to the
coast as is safe. Bypass the actual headland
of Grut Ness and descend to the rocky

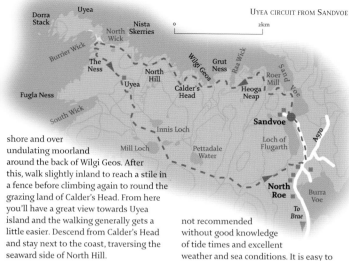

shore and over undulating moorland around the back of Wilgi Geos. After this, walk slightly inland to reach a stile in a fence before climbing again to round the grazing land of Calder's Head. From here you'll have a great view towards Uyea island and the walking generally gets a little easier. Descend from Calder's Head and stay next to the coast, traversing the seaward side of North Hill.

At the back of an inlet cross the fence to stay on the seaward side which has some spectacular views but also needs care near the steep drops. Alternatively the fence can be avoided by heading inland to a track which can be followed to the right to the house at Uyea, from which you can aim northwest through gates to reach Uyea island; however, this approach misses out the amazing scenery of the final approach. If continuing on the coast you'll eventually pass to the north of a small lochan and Uyea island will start to come into view. Pass the lovely sandy beach of North Wick to reach The Ness above the narrow tidal crossing point to Uyea.

It is possible to descend the steep and slippery path between the two fences and cross the sands at very low tide, but the sea is very treacherous here and this is not recommended without good knowledge of tide times and excellent weather and sea conditions. It is easy to become stranded. Instead bear south to explore the cliffs of The Ness and enjoy views of Uyea.

When you are ready to return aim southeast, crossing the cropped grass to a gate in the fence. Then follow a faint grassy track to another gate leading to the track just southwest of the isolated crofthouse at Uyea. Turn right, going through the gate and, as the track climbs, ignore a right turn and continue through the increasingly barren and rocky landscape. After two more gates the route passes between two lochans where you may spot red-throated divers. The green grazing land as the track descends towards North Roe and the Loch of Flugarth comes as a welcome relief. At the road turn left and left again to return on the minor road to the starting point at Sandvoe.

◂ Beach with Uyea in the background

Lunna Ness and the Stanes of Stofast

Distance 11km **Time** 4 hours
Terrain pathless moorland, rough and
boggy in places, stiles, navigation skills
needed **Map** OS Explorer 468
Access no public transport to the start

Explore the moorland peninsula of Lunna
Ness, visiting the gigantic Stanes of
Stofast before reaching the headland and
returning along a coastline which is home
to otters and seals.

The walk starts near the road end at
Outrabister. To get here take the road
through Lunna to the parking area on the
right-hand side just before the private road
sign. Begin by walking back along the road
away from the croft at Outrabister, keeping
to the road and ignoring two stiles signed
for the Stanes of Stofast. After passing the
houses at Heog and Hamnavoe and the
long natural spit below them take a track
on the left signed 'access route' opposite a

ruined building. Once through the gate
follow the track uphill, passing through
another gate. The freshwater Loch of
Grutwick is near the track, which becomes
grassy as it descends towards the pebbly
beach at Grut Wick.

After exploring the beach head north
along the coast, climbing to stay near the
clifftops before descending to cross a burn
and a boggy area of ground between two
hillocks slightly inland. Keep the small
lochan on your left and stay to the right of
a very wet area, then climb to overlook the
South Loch of Stofast with the Stanes of
Stofast on the horizon beyond.

If these look out of place, it's because
they are. Dragged here by a glacier during
the last ice age, the rocks were originally a
single 2000-tonne erratic boulder which
has been split by frost over time. Skirt
around the west side of the loch and
detour to the massive stanes before

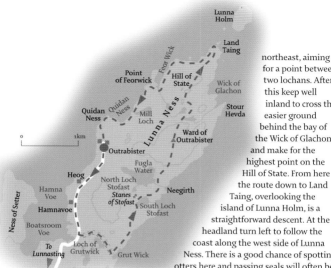

northeast, aiming for a point between two lochans. After this keep well inland to cross the easier ground behind the bay of the Wick of Glachon and make for the highest point on the Hill of State. From here the route down to Land Taing, overlooking the island of Lunna Holm, is a straightforward descent. At the headland turn left to follow the coast along the west side of Lunna Ness. There is a good chance of spotting otters here and passing seals will often be keeping a watchful eye on you as well.

The inlet of Feor Wick is a good place to spot eider ducks and seals. Continuing along the coast, bypass the Point of Feorwick and then cross the outflow of Mill Loch near the shore. The ruins of an old grain mill are still visible on the watercourse. Cross a stile and head round the back of Riven Noust. After another stile keep close to the coast on the short turf of Quidan Ness. Look out for the crofthouse at Outrabister and once it comes into view head diagonally inland across boggy ground to go through a gate between the house and a large shed. This leads almost immediately through another gate. Turn left to return to the parking area.

returning to the water to continue the walk. From the far end of the loch aim northeast over a low shoulder and continue ahead veering slightly inland to reach a stile over a stone wall just east of Fugla Water. Bear northeast to climb the heather moorland, then more directly north as the ground steepens, aiming for the summit of Ward of Outrabister. This is the highest point on the peninsula at 90m and, despite its diminutive height, there are good views from the trig point across the interior of Lunna Ness to the south and over the water to Burravoe on Yell to the north.

Head north downhill at first and then

Out Skerries: Bruray and Housay

Distance 11.75km **Time** 5 hours
Terrain pathless, some rough ground,
stiles **Map** OS Explorer 468 **Access** ferry
from Vidlin on Mainland Shetland, or
from Laxo via Whalsay; occasionally from
Lerwick. Air link from Tingwall Airport

**Take the memorable trip to the remote
archipelago of Out Skerries for this
circular walk which explores the two
connected islands of Housay and Bruray.
It can be completed as a daytrip between
ferries or flights on certain days.**

A trip to Skerries needs both advance
planning and the willingness to be flexible
as sea conditions and weather frequently
dictate the transport options. The ferry
journey to the most easterly islands of
Shetland can be notoriously rough. This
walk starts from the ferry terminal pier on
Bruray, but can also be picked up

en route from the airstrip if flying.
The pier is sheltered by a magnificent
natural harbour lying at the heart of the
islands, with entrances to both the south
and northeast. Start the walk by heading
towards the houses, immediately turning
right to pass between a bungalow on the
left and some sheds and works on the
right to reach the shoreline. Turn left for
the first part of the walk, going anti-
clockwise around the coast of Bruray.

The fine lighthouse seen across the
straits on Bound Skerry is the tallest in
Shetland; adjacent to it is the now
uninhabited isle of Grunay, where the
lighthouse keepers once lived. Climb a stile
over a fence and then keep straight on to
reach a gate, passing the airstrip. As the
route rounds the back of a shingle bay
keep an eye open for eider ducks. At the far
end is a ruin and the ground rises to a
rocky headland known as the Head of
Bloshin – which can either be climbed or
bypassed by staying on the grassier ground
to the left.

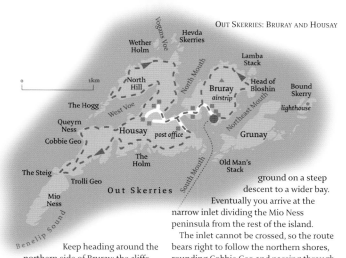

Keep heading around the northern side of Bruray; the cliffs start to rise and the going becomes rougher. At the back of a deep inlet, or geo, the highest point of Out Skerries at 53m can be reached by a short detour of a few hundred metres. Otherwise keep going until you reach a fence and gate. Once on the far side aim left downhill and pass to the right of a small lochan. Turn right when you reach the road and go past the school on the way to the bridge linking Bruray to the larger island of Housay.

Climb the hill beyond, branching left at a fork to pass a tiny shop and post office and reach the house at the end of the road. Keep to the left of this house to begin the clockwise circumnavigation of Housay. The rocky easterly point can be bypassed and from just beyond it bear west along the southern coast of the island, staying as near to the coast as possible but detouring inland around geos and to find easier ground on a steep descent to a wider bay.

Eventually you arrive at the narrow inlet dividing the Mio Ness peninsula from the rest of the island.

The inlet cannot be crossed, so the route bears right to follow the northern shores, rounding Cobbie Geo and passing through a gap in a stone wall to reach Queyrn Ness and then alongside the sheltered waters of West Voe. Keep close to the shore, going through gaps in walls where necessary. Once near the houses go right to a stile over a larger wall and then carry straight on, aiming to the right of a shed. Cross a track via two stiles and keep following the shore, eventually rounding the head of West Voe and soon crossing rougher ground on the north side, passing above an old kailyard. Pass a lochan and skirt round the north side of North Hill with ever-more impressive cliff scenery before finally descending to the shingle beach at Vogans Voe.

Keep following the shore to a fence which is crossed via a stile on the right before returning to the coast. After a stile and a gate pass a fish farm to reach the road. Turn left to return to the start.

◀ Bruray harbour

45

Muckle Roe and the Hams

Distance 11.5km **Time** 5 hours
Terrain pathless, rough-going in places,
track, navigation skills needed
Map OS Explorer 469 **Access** no public
transport to the start

The spectacular coastline of Muckle Roe
is rated by many Shetlanders as the finest
walk in the archipelago. Muckle Roe is
connected to Mainland Shetland by a
bridge. Much of this route is rugged,
but the effort is richly rewarded by
fantastic scenery.

Just before the road end at Little-ayre
there is a parking area on the left. Start by
walking along the road, following it as it
curves up to the right at the end. Turn left
through a gate onto a track (signed for
Lighthouse and the Hams). In a grassy
field leave the track where it bends,
following the sign for the lighthouse to go
through a walkers' gate. A good path leads

to the beautiful beach of Muckle Ayre.

Don't take the path above the cliffs
immediately at the far end of the beach;
instead head to the right to join a clear
path which cuts back left across the slope
higher up. A short boggy section leads over
Burki Hill but soon the path improves as it
crosses the heather slope. Cross two stiles
and stay on the path which has a metal
handrail for one section. Descend to Gilsa
Water, a lovely hill lochan, and then aim
diagonally up the slope beyond to
a high point. On the descent look out for
the dramatic blowhole of the Hole of
Hellier just to the left – but don't approach
it too closely!

Continue downhill, making for the
lighthouse ahead. Follow a line of
fenceposts after the back of an inlet to
detour to the lighthouse where there are
amazing views of the coastline. Seals are

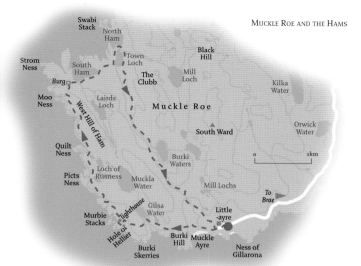

often hauled out on the rocks below here. The next section of the route is pathless and extremely rugged: keep well back from the cliff edge and work your way around any rocky crags, eventually reaching the west side of the Loch of Rusness. Here a vague path can be picked up and the terrain becomes a little easier as the route continues along the cliffs and around more inlets. Keep to the right of a fence and further on cross a stile, staying above the cliffs. Near here a sea stack supported on two natural arches can be seen.

After a further stile you reach a ruined house at Burg. This area is known as the Hams with the name deriving from the Norse for harbour. It is said that South Ham was once a centre for smuggling from the Faroes. From Burg go down to a gate and a track. When the track turns inland

leave it to continue along the southern shore of the South Ham. Go over a stile and at the next bay take a faint grassy track leading up a shallow glen. Soon this reaches a vehicle track; turn left along it to the breathtakingly beautiful bay of North Ham surrounded by high cliffs.

Cross the pebbly ground to the north of Town Loch to pick up an old track that returns along its eastern shores. Up the burn is an old Norse mill, but this route continues along the faint track to reach some more abandoned houses. Here the track peters out; cross grassy ground to reach a modern farm shed. From here a gravel vehicle track leads south, climbing up over the moors to cross the central part of Muckle Roe – a real contrast to the rest of the walk. This eventually takes you back to the start.

◄ Ruin at South Ham

47

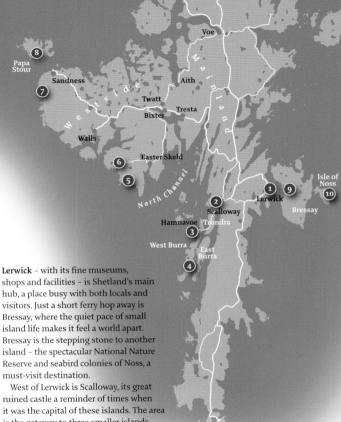

Voe

Mainland

Papa Stour

8

Sandness 7

Aith

Twatt

Tresta

Bixter

Walls

Easter Skeld

6

5

North Channel

Isle of Noss

10

2

Lerwick 1 9

Scalloway

Hamnavoe

Trondra

Bressay

3

West Burra

East Burra

4

Lerwick – with its fine museums, shops and facilities – is Shetland's main hub, a place busy with both locals and visitors. Just a short ferry hop away is Bressay, where the quiet pace of small island life makes it feel a world apart. Bressay is the stepping stone to another island – the spectacular National Nature Reserve and seabird colonies of Noss, a must-visit destination.

West of Lerwick is Scalloway, its great ruined castle a reminder of times when it was the capital of these islands. The area is the gateway to three smaller islands linked by bridges – West and East Burra, and Trondra.

Further from Lerwick is Westside, an area little known to outsiders but boasting arguably the most dramatic cliff scenery in all Shetland – which is saying a lot!

Off the coast is the fragile island community of Papa Stour. Whilst this looks low-lying at first glance, a closer exploration reveals an array of remarkable arches, stacks and sea caves.

Easthouse Heritage Centre ▶

Central Mainland, Papa Stour, Bressay and Noss

Lerwick explorer

Distance 6km Time 2 hours
Terrain pavements and surfaced
footpaths Map OS Explorer 466
Access buses from all over Shetland, ferry
from Aberdeen/Orkney

Explore both the buildings and
coastal scenery of Lerwick, including
an impressive restored Iron Age broch.
The perfect introduction to the capital
of Shetland, you could easily spend a day
on this route, combining it with a visit to
the museum, shops and eating
opportunities nearby.

The walk starts from Victoria Car Park
(charge) on the seafront at Lerwick and is
easily reached from anywhere in the town.
Leave the car park and turn left along the
front, with Bressay Sound on your left.
Lerwick grew up in the 17th century with
the start of the herring fishing industry,
which was largely run at that time by the
Dutch. Worries about the extent of foreign
influence led to the building of the fort

visited near the end of this walk, around
which the town then expanded with
some of the older buildings dating back
to the 1700s.

Head along the front and turn up the
alley between the RNLI building and the
Queen's Hotel. Turn left along the
pedestrianised street and onto the back
road beyond. The old buildings backing
onto the water are known as the Lodberries
and one of them may be familiar as the
home of Detective Jimmy Perez in the BBC
crime drama *Shetland*. Keep on the road
nearest to the sea, soon rising and passing
a garage which has the old Foula mailboat
for its roof. Follow the signs for The Knab,
a rocky coastal outcrop which is now
reached by turning left onto a surfaced
path before the cemetery.

Keep close to the coastline, passing some
World War II defences and with good views
across the sound to Bressay. The walled
path climbs to a fine viewpoint
overlooking The Knab. Follow the tarmac

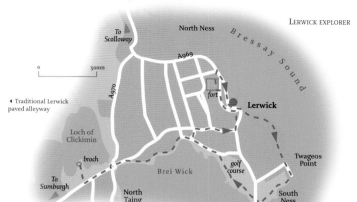

◄ Traditional Lerwick paved alleyway

lane inland, then immediately turn left through a gate to follow a path along the left edge of the golf course. When this reaches Breiwick Road turn left and, when the road turns right, go through the walkers' gate ahead and onto the coastal path. At South Road turn left and carefully cross the roundabout to reach, on the far side, the A970 towards Sumburgh, keeping on the right-hand side of the road. Follow this until a signed path on the right indicates the way to Clickimin Broch. Although heavily restored, this 2000-year-old defensive structure gives an excellent introduction to brochs and is in a lovely position overlooking the loch.

From the broch return along South Road and the coastal path to Breiwick Road and carry on up this to King Harald Street where you turn left. When you reach the main Scalloway Road turn right towards the town centre. At a mini roundabout keep left to head down a paved alleyway which emerges onto Commercial Street, Lerwick's pedestrianised shopping street.

Turn left here, soon passing the Merkat Cross. Continue along Commercial Street, then turn left up a lane (signed Fort Charlotte) before it becomes open to traffic. Enter the fort by taking the archway on the right. There are information boards explaining the history of the site and some good views available from the stronghold's walls. To leave head across the parking area with the grass to your right and go through the arch at the far end. Turn right and then immediately left, before going right again to end up on the main road that leads back to the right along Lerwick's seafront. After a couple of commercial buildings on the left side, pass the Bressay ferry terminal. To the left is where the Viking Squad gathers with its wooden galley at the start of each year's Up Helly Aa, Europe's largest fire festival and a celebration of the old New Year. Continue along the front to return to the car park.

Scalloway and Bur Wick

Distance 6.75km Time 3 hours
Terrain minor roads, tracks, short section
of rough pathless coastal walking
Map OS Explorer 466 Access good bus
service from Lerwick to Scalloway

From the ancient capital of Shetland
with its imposing ruined castle, take a
tour of the coast to the west of the town
and the bay of Bur Wick.

Start from the Burn Beach Car Park on
the seafront in the centre of Scalloway,
where there are public toilets. The ancient
capital of Shetland, Scalloway has been
used as an important harbour since the
Vikings came here in the 9th century and
it remains the second largest settlement
on Shetland today. The town's historic
importance is expressed by the large
ancient house with stone carvings
above the doorway which looms over
the car park.

Leaving the car park, turn left along
Main Street to walk through the old town.
Soon you reach a memorial to the
Shetland Bus, the clandestine operation
to transport goods and prisoners of war
from German-occupied Norway during
World War II. Crossings were usually made
in small fishing boats under cover of
darkness. Conditions far out in the
North Sea without any lights under
constant threat of discovery by German
patrols must have been grim. Several of
the boats were attacked and sunk with
the loss of many lives.

Pass the marina and go around the bay –
there are good views back to Scalloway and
its castle. Stay on the road as it passes the
Marine Centre of the University of the
Highlands and Islands and curves right,
climbing towards the houses of Port
Arthur. At the bend take the second
turning on the left and soon go through a

gate onto a private road towards the coast. The island of Trondra can be seen across the water, linked to Mainland by a bridge.

When the surfaced road ends at a waterworks, continue on a rough track above the Pund Voe. The track fades and the small lighthouse on the Point of the Pund with good views to West Burra can be reached by a short detour. Otherwise bear right along the coast, following the low cliffs as the going gets much rougher and largely pathless. The route climbs across heather above the sea before descending to the bay at Shalder's Ayre.

After another bay the cliffs get steeper; take care on the airy sheep path or climb directly uphill to avoid it. After the steep ground the going eases and the houses on the other side of Bur Wick come into view. Go through a gap near the seaward end of the drystane dyke and keep ahead to reach a rough track. Turn right along this to climb in zigzags to the top of the Hill of Houlland, with great views back over Bur Wick. Cross the cattle grid and ignore a track going right, instead heading downhill, with views over Scalloway. Eventually go through a gate and past farm buildings to join a minor road. Turn right

to return to the town, then turn left on Lovers Lane to reach New Road, which leads on to the car park.

Before ending the walk carry on along this road to visit Scalloway Castle, built by the Second Earl of Orkney, Partrick Stewart, between 1600 and 1607. Although his main home was Birsay Palace on Orkney, a Shetland residence was needed when he became de facto ruler over this archipelago as well. His rule was short-lived, however, as complaints by Shetland lairds led to Stewart's execution in 1615 in Edinburgh. The castle today is ruined, but still stands to four storeys and is open to the public.

◀ Looking over Scalloway Harbour and Castle

Meal Beach and Hamnavoe

Distance 4.5km **Time** 2 hours
Terrain path with stiles through grazing
land (dogs to be kept under tight control);
rockier underfoot on optional detour to
lighthouse **Map** OS Explorer 466
Access bus from Scalloway to Hamnavoe

**Cross one of central Shetland's finest
sandy beaches at the start of this
short coastal excursion, visiting the
Fugla Ness Lighthouse and the village
of Hamnavoe.**

West Burra is reached via a bridge from
the island of Trondra; itself linked by a
bridge to Mainland. The walk starts at the
car park and toilets at Meal. Follow the
signed path opposite the car park to the
beach – a sheltered crescent of fine white
sand and a good place for a swim on a hot
day (with a wetsuit in more usual
temperatures). Cross to the far side of the
beach and climb the rocks, going over a

stile in a fence. Continue round the
coastline to Urmlee shingle beach. Here
the path crosses the remains of noosts –
depressions cut into the turf at the back of
the beach, where boats were once hauled
up and secured. Stay on the edge of the
shingle, ignoring a stile on the right, and at
the far end of the beach climb a stile
straight ahead. Head up to another stile
and after this bear left to continue above
the low cliffs of Lu Ness.

From Lu Ness the coast leads to
the small headland of Biargar, crossing
another stile along the way. From the
headland aim north, climbing to reach a
stile over a fence with a gate just to the
right. Go over the stile and bear left – or
northwest – downhill to a further stile.
Here archaeologists have discovered
the remains of Neolithic houses, burnt
mounds and an underground souterrain
which dates back 6000 years. As you

Crossing the white sands of Meal Beach ▼

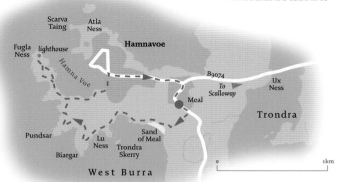

Scarva
Taing
Atla
Ness

Hamnavoe

Fugla
Ness   *lighthouse*

Hanna Voe

B9074

To
Scalloway

Meal

Ux
Ness

Trondra

Pundsar

Lu
Ness

Sand
of Meal

Trondra
Skerry

Biargar

West Burra

0   1km

cross the low ground in front, the small lighthouse at Fugla Ness can be seen ahead.

The approach to the lighthouse crosses some very rocky ground on a narrow strip of land. Just continue around the coast if you want to avoid crossing the rocks. Otherwise the small lighthouse is a lovely place to stop and look out for otters or other passing wildlife. Return from the lighthouse and continue towards

Hamnavoe, climbing a stile to follow an indistinct path. This becomes clearer as it nears the marina and a section of boardwalk leads to the village. Take the route up between two houses and turn left along the road, and then right at the main road to head uphill through Hamnavoe. Be sure to look out for the unusual shell-covered building on the left. Take the next turn on the right signed for Papil to return to the starting point.

Banna Minn and Kettla Ness

**Distance 7.75km Time 3 hours
Terrain pathless coast, wet underfoot
in places, some fence crossings with no
stiles Map OS Explorer 466 Access bus
from Scalloway to Papil, just under 1km
from the start**

**Banna Minn is one of Shetland's most
iconic beaches – a narrow tombolo of
white sand leading out onto the Kettla
Ness peninsula. Explore the wild coastline
beyond on this stunning circuit.**

The walk starts from the parking area
which is signed for Minn beach, found at
the end of the road south through West
Burra, just beyond Papil. The thatched
cottage passed just before the car park is
Easthouse, a crofthouse restored by the

Burra History Group and now open as a
heritage centre. Follow the track south,
soon looking ahead to the beach. Cross the
tombolo with the fine sands to your right,
then continue to the far end of the beach
and climb the stile.

Now aim right to begin an anti-clockwise
circuit of the peninsula. Stay to the right of
the beach cottage and round the Lotra of
Minn with great views northwards to Virda
across the Banna Minn. Head left to go
round a fence on the clifftop and then
carry on along the short turf, soon passing
chunky Fugla Stack. This basalt stack was
the scene of a shipwreck when the steel
steamship *The Castor* ran aground with the
loss of all crew in February 1910. The winch,
engines, propeller shaft and stern gear still

lie on the seabed, sometimes visited by divers. It was known locally as the 'Sweetie Wreck' due to the many tins of peppermints that were washed ashore.

Continue climbing towards a hill topped by a cairn, crossing a stile over a fence just before you reach the summit. From here keep the cliffs on your right as the walk leads towards the southernmost part of West Burra. Stay to the right of a small lochan to reach The Heugg peninsula. Make your way onto this, descending slightly and crossing a rocky area to detour to the cairn, enjoying the views back to the cliffs and caves. Now head round the gentler Kettla Ness, staying to the right of

another lochan before climbing a low hill which makes up the southernmost part of West Burra. From here you can expect grand views down the coast towards the southern tip of Mainland, dominated by the mighty cliffs of Fitful Head.

Return along the lower cliffs of the eastern coastline with views across to East Burra. There are a couple of low wire fences with no stiles that need to be carefully stepped over. Eventually some ruined buildings are passed before the route returns to the tombolo and Minn beach, where it's now a simple case of dragging yourself away from the perfect sand to return to the start.

◀ Minn beach tombolo

Westerwick coast from Silwick

Distance 8.5km Time 3 hours 30
Terrain pathless, grassy clifftops, some
fences without stiles, navigation skills
needed Map OS Explorer 467
Access no public transport to the start

Boasting an abundance of spectacular
coastal scenery, this walk has some of
the most impressive sea stacks, natural
arches and caves to be found anywhere in
the British Isles.

Start from the end of the public road in
Silwick; if parking take care not to block
access or the turning circle which is used
by large farm vehicles. Walk through the
gate on the track and immediately branch
left on a grassy track, aiming for a gate. Go
through this and continue until you reach
the coast at the back of a deep geo; Berga
Stack can be seen by looking down into it.

Bear right to begin walking along the
mostly grassy cliff edge as an amazing
array of coastal scenery comes into view.
Erne's Stack and its neighbours loom like
jagged mountains straight from the sea.
Cross a fence to the left of a corner post,
where there are dramatic views directly
down to a tiny beach in the shadow of the
stacks. After passing a more isolated stack,
the Skerry of the Wick, keep heading round
the coast, crossing another fence, and
continue out to the next headland,
descending and then climbing a little to
reach yet another amazing viewpoint.

The route now goes up the west side of
the headland, climbing to pass above a
geo. Cross the next fence at a stile and aim
towards Westerwick, going through a gate
in the corner of the field to the right of the
old stone building by the shore. Pass

◄ Erne's Stack

through a walkers' gate alongside the building and drop downhill to cross the burn. Take the grassy track on the far side to climb through a gateway, bearing inland and uphill to reach a minor road. Follow this to the left to a turning area and go left over a stile. Cross the field to a walkers' gate at the far corner and keep climbing uphill with the fence on your left. Carry on through more gates and a stile to reach the unfenced cliffs and continue to the next headland where there are more stunning views and further sea stacks. Detour around the deep geo with an arch in the wall that cuts north towards Lambi Loch.

Continue onto the Nev and northwards along the coast, climbing a low fence before the ascent to Drongi Field, from the top of which you can retrace your steps back to this point. From here bear ESE across the moorland, aiming to return to a fence just north of a small lochan. Go over this and now retrace the outward route downhill to Westerwick and beyond to the stile on the east side of Wester Wick Bay. From here walk uphill over the moorland with the fence on your left. Go through a sliding gate at the top fence corner and continue with the fence to your left to reach a cattle shed. From here head down the track to return to the start.

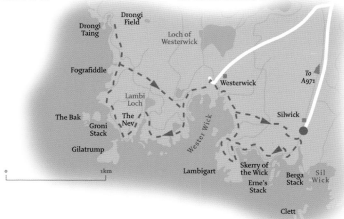

Broch of Culswick and the Burga Stacks

**Distance 6km Time 2 hours 30
Terrain track, coastal walking, boggy in
places, navigation skills needed
Map OS Explorer 467 Access no public
transport to the start**

**This relatively short coastal circuit
packs a real punch with its awesome
cliff scenery, ancient broch, sea stacks
and inland loch.**

Start from Culswick, around 200m before
the end of the road, taking the track
through a farm gate westwards uphill
(a long-gone telephone box is marked on
OS maps here). There is very limited
parking near the sign for Culswick
Methodist Chapel, but take care not to
block any entrances. When the track forks
keep right, passing through a farm gate.

A short detour up to the right can be
made to visit the very simple, atmospheric
and remote chapel. Otherwise carry on
ahead, going through another gate and
ignoring the track heading up to the
wind turbines.

The route descends to the shore of the
Loch of Sotersta with the ruins of the
settlement of Sotersta just about visible
to the south. The track skirts the loch and,
as it climbs, offers good views of the
impressive Westerwick cliffs in the
distance over to the left. Keep on the main
track and soon a smaller loch comes into
view with the prominent remains of Broch
of Culswick beyond. Just before the track
starts to rise, turn left – a short way
beyond a marker post – to follow a
sometimes wet footpath diagonally left
across the hillock to a stony causeway at
the outflow of the loch. Cross this and,

◀ Broch of Culswick

beyond the gate, make your way up the steep ground ahead to reach the broch.

The broch is around 2000 years old, but parts of its walls still stand to around 3m high, including a huge triangular lintel stone over the entrance. This is a great vantage point, with views northwest across the water to Vaila and the stacks and islands in between. To get an even better view bear north from the broch to look over the cliffs and into Gruting Voe. Otherwise start the coastal section of the walk by heading south along the clifftops which soon rise as the scenery becomes even more impressive.

As the cliffs rise and a ramshackle stile crosses a fence, there are views of the Burga Stacks, one of which is reputed to have been inhabited by a monk or hermit who received supplies hauled up in a bucket.

Stay on the clifftop until you reach the headland known as The Nev – another great vantage point. From here the route turns inland, heading for a gate in a fence near the small lochan. To reach it take a diagonal line to the left, bearing NNW and aiming just to the right of the lochan. Go through the gate and continue in the same direction to reach the outward track. Turn right along the track to follow it back to the start at Culswick.

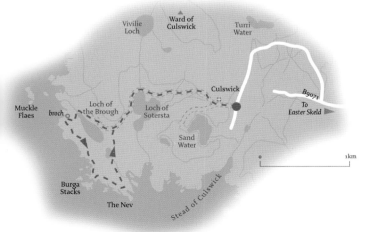

Sandness Hill and the Bay of Deepdale

Distance 10.75km **Time** 5 hours
Terrain very rough pathless moorland
and clifftop, wet and steep in places,
navigation skills needed
Map OS Explorer 467 **Access** occasional
bus between Sandness and Walls (but bus
times make it impossible to do the walk
and return the same day)

This challenging coast and moorland
circuit offers a wild slice of Shetland's
west coast before climbing to a high
summit and returning over peaty
moorland and rough pastures, home
to hardy Shetland ponies.

The best place to park is where the
Netherdale road turns off at Dale of Walls.
From here follow the road towards
Netherdale, soon branching left onto a
track leading down towards the Voe of

Dale. When the track swings left, fork
right onto a smaller track to reach the
back of the bay. Cross the pebbly shoreline
and climb up the far side, going through a
gap in a fence. Now aim left to head along
the coastline, making a gently rising
traverse across the pathless but easy
slopes. Soon the chunky stack known as
the Clett comes into view.

Continue climbing as the cliffs increase
in height. You can choose to shortcut
across the tip of the Mu Ness peninsula
and rejoin the clifftops on the northern
side. There are stunning views along the
coast to the dramatic stacks, arches and
cliffs of Weinnia Ness. At a fence bear right
to reach and cross a stile before dropping
downhill to a junction of fences and

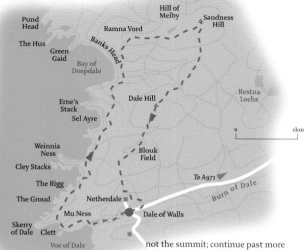

another stile; it is usually wet underfoot here. Cross a couple more stiles to reach an unfenced stretch of coast. Round the cliffs of Sel Ayre and continue until you are looking down onto the Bay of Deepdale. Well named, Deepdale is both deep and extremely steep – walk a little way inland until you can safely descend one of the grassy gullies (great care is needed) and cross the burn. What goes down must go up and so it is now necessary to climb, again steeply at first but easing as the route continues around the cliffs of Banks Head opposite Ramna Vord.

From here head inland over Ramna Vord towards Sandness Hill. The large cairn is not the summit; continue past more cairns to reach the trig point and a final smaller cairn, where there are extensive views with Papa Stour and Foula particularly well seen on a clear day. Start the return walk by aiming south and then southwest, edging around any deep-looking peat hags to reach Dale Hill and then Blouk Field. Keep aiming southwest; eventually passing through a gate in the fence. From here, look across the valley and aim in the same direction as the bend in the road leading to Walls. Go over a couple of stiles as you descend, bearing a little to the left for a third stile and then cross a fourth before going left down towards the burn. After a further stile you reach a footbridge over a burn. Cross this and bear right to reach the road, where you turn right to return to the start.

Coastal circuit of Papa Stour

Distance 17km **Time 6 hours 30**
Terrain pathless, rough coastal
walking, navigation skills needed
Map OS Explorer 467 **Access ferry to Papa**
Stour from West Burrafirth – booking
essential; regular flight from Tingwall

**What could be more satisfying than a
circumnavigation on foot of the remote
island of Papa Stour, taking in high cliffs,
massive sea arches and caves, as well as
the island's highest point.**

The ferry doesn't run every day so this
walk is only possible on certain days of the
week if you're not staying on the island.
As the walk is long and remote, ensure the
weather is good and that there is plenty of
time to complete the route – which can be
cut short at a couple of places. From the
jetty head uphill, passing the waiting room
and toilet building and continue straight
on, ignoring the turn to Hurdiback.

After passing a house at Da Biggins look
out for the partially reconstructed
medieval Norse house, or stofa, on the
right-hand side. Continue until just before
the church and take the track on the left.
Alternatively, detour to the kirk to see the
beautiful stained glass window created in
memory of the six men from Papa Stour
who lost their lives in World War I. After a
short distance take the walkers' gate on the
right and then aim right just before the
sands onto a path leading to a stile. Carry
on along the coast, keeping on the seaward
side of a fence after another stile to pass a
sandy bay. The route now stays close to the
coast, crossing stiles at each fence. Beyond
a large blowhole with a natural arch the
route climbs to a high point on the coast
to the southwest of the airstrip.

The next landmark is the remains of a
hill dyke which marked the ownership
boundary between two lairds in the 18th

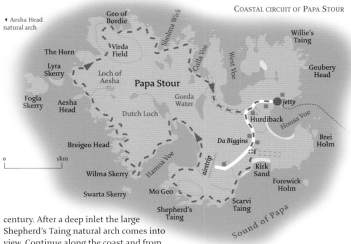

◄ Aesha Head natural arch

Geo of Bordie · Sholma Wick · Willie's Taing · The Horn · Virda Field · Culla Voe · West Voe · Geubery Head · Lyra Skerry · Loch of Aesha · Papa Stour · jetty · Fogla Skerry · Aesha Head · Gorda Water · Hurdiback · Housa Voe · Brei Holm · Dutch Loch · Da Biggins · Breigeo Head · airstrip · Kirk Sand · Hamna Voe · Wilma Skerry · Forewick Holm · Swarta Skerry · Mo Geo · Scarvi Taing · Shepherd's Taing · Sound of Papa

0 ___ 1km

century. After a deep inlet the large Shepherd's Taing natural arch comes into view. Continue along the coast and from the back of Mo Geo, shortcut north to reach the shore of Hamna Voe. Cross the heather moorland, passing ruins of boat shelters and kailyards. At the far end of the voe the ruins of a series of grain mills can be seen on the small watercourse. Cross the burn and keep close to the far side of the voe to reach the ruins of a shoreside house after a gate.

The coastline becomes much more dramatic as the cliffs return with a selection of skerries, stacks and natural arches, including the high jagged stack at Breigeo. Head slightly inland to pass around the far side of Kirstan Hol, a large collapsed sea cave with a smaller sibling just inland. Keep close to the cliffs before descending to the shore as Aesha Stack appears ahead, with a keyhole cut out of it and a huge arch through the headland just beyond. Pass the headland, with the

islands of Fogla Skerry and Lyra Skerry beyond, and the high sea stack of Snolda. Then bypass the Horn headland by aiming directly for the summit of Virda Field, the highest point on the island, from the back of Akers Geo.

From here you can take a more direct route back to the start by following a faint path southeast. Otherwise continue by bearing northwest past the remains of a coastguard lookout and a cairn, before aiming north to the cliffs and heading around the Geo of Bordie. Continue towards Sholma Wick, with a sea arch on its far side. Cross a fence and then cut across the next headland to reach the low inlet of Culla Voe. Keep on the seaward side of a fence to round the voe and then take a rough track heading inland. At a junction carry straight on and turn left at the road to return to the ferry jetty.

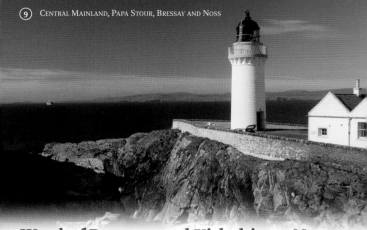

Ward of Bressay and Kirkabister Ness

Distance 12.5km **Time** 5 hours
Terrain minor roads, tracks, pathless
boggy moorland **Map** OS Explorer 466
Access regular ferries from Lerwick

**If the hustle and bustle of Lerwick
gets too much, just hop on the ferry to
explore the Isle of Bressay on this circuit
taking in the highest point, the Ward
of Bressay, before returning via a
stunningly-situated lighthouse.**

Take the ferry from Lerwick and start the
walk from the Bressay ferry terminal where
there are toilets and parking. Follow the
road away from the jetty and keep right at
a junction (signed for Kirkabister, Noss and
Mail). Ignore a turn on the left for
Gunnista and stay on the road as it nears
the coast and passes a marina. The masts
which sit atop the Ward of Bressay can be
seen clearly up to the left. Pass a church

and stay on the road as it curves left away
from the coast. Turn right at a staggered
crossroads opposite the shop (signed for
Glebe and Kirkabister).

Ignore a right turn near the houses and
turn left immediately after the playpark.
Beyond some sheds the route becomes a
track, crosses a cattle grid and begins to
climb the Ward of Bressay. Keep on the
main track all the way to the masts at the
summit, the highest point on the island,
which is marked by a trig point to the right
of the buildings. The views across the
Sound and over to Lerwick are superb.

The easiest way back is simply to retrace
your steps. However, the circuit can be
continued from here over very rough and
peat-hagged moorland. Stay on the track to
the right of the summit buildings and
then strike out southeast over the
pathless, tussocked and peaty moorland

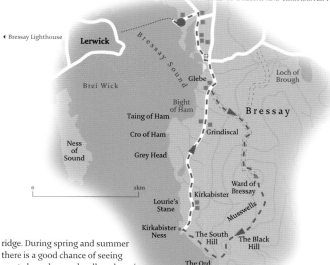

◄ Bressay Lighthouse

Lerwick

Bressay Sound

Glebe

Brei Wick

Bight of Ham

Loch of Brough

Bressay

Taing of Ham

Cro of Ham

Grindiscal

Ness of Sound

Grey Head

Ward of Bressay

0   2km

Kirkabister

Lourie's Stane

Musswells

Kirkabister Ness

The South Hill

The Black Hill

The Ord

ridge. During spring and summer there is a good chance of seeing great skuas, known locally as bonxies, which nest nearby and can be very aggressive towards unwary walkers. It is a joy, however, to watch their graceful flight and before they have chicks you can sometimes get a good close-up view of them on the ground.

Keep to the highest land as the route descends, eventually bearing southwest over Musswells and Black Hill. Head straight over a track and up to South Hill before descending south to the top of the cliffs above The Ord, near a huge drystane dyke – thankfully the end of the boggy section. Now the going improves as the route descends alongside a fence to the right and goes through a gate.

The Bressay Lighthouse, perched above an impressive natural arch on Kirkabister

Ness, soon comes into view. Keep going down the slope, aiming right as you approach the lighthouse to pass through a gate and reach the public road. The lighthouse protects the entrance to Lerwick Harbour and was designed and built by David and Thomas of the famous Stevenson family between 1856 and 1858, one of four lighthouses built in Shetland by the brothers. It was replaced in 2012 by a light operated by Lerwick Port Authority.

To return to the ferry take the road heading north which climbs away from the lighthouse. After 3km the road reaches the cluster of houses at the Glebe, from where the outward route can be followed back to the ferry terminal at the start.

Isle of Noss

Distance 8.25km **Time** 4 hours 30
Terrain coastal path, wet in places, high
unprotected cliffs **Map** OS Explorer 467
Access ferry to Noss from the Isle of
Bressay (via ferry from Lerwick); no public
transport to the Noss ferry

**If you are a birdwatcher, the Isle of Noss is
simply unmissable. This circuit takes in
the soaring cliffs, home to a vast gannet
colony and many puffins, as well as a fine
sandy beach and a coastline which is a
hotspot for cetaceans.**

The National Nature Reserve of Noss lies
off the far side of Bressay, itself an island
just east of Lerwick. Bressay is accessible via
a short vehicle ferry, but before leaving
Lerwick check that the tiny inflatable boat
over to Noss is running that day. Although
it operates from late April to late August
every day except Monday and Thursday,
even a small swell can prevent it crossing
the narrows to Noss. It is possible to walk

across Bressay to reach the parking area for
the Noss boat on the far side of the island,
but this would add another 10km and a
sizeable hill to the day. If driving, park at
the top of the descent to the jetty where
there is an information board, and then
walk down the final rough track. A red flag
flying on Noss indicates that the boat isn't
running that day.

Noss is managed by Scottish Natural
Heritage and after you land a warden will
usually introduce you to the island and let
you know about any seasonal changes to
the preferred walking route. There is also
a small visitor centre and a list of recent
wildlife sightings.

This route heads anti-clockwise around
the island; start by walking past the front
of the house and go left to pass the pony
pund, an enclosure built by the Marquis of
Londonderry in 1870 for breeding the
Shetland ponies needed for his coal mines
in County Durham. Go through a gap in

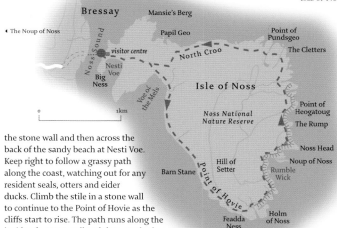

Bressay

Mansie's Berg

Papil Geo

Point of Pundsgeo

◀ The Noup of Noss

visitor centre

North Croo

The Cletters

Nesti Voe

Big Ness

Voe of the Mels

Isle of Noss

Point of Heogatoug

0   1km

Noss National Nature Reserve

The Rump

Noss Head

Hill of Setter

Barn Stane

Point of Hovie

Noup of Noss

Rumble Wick

Feadda Ness

Holm of Noss

the stone wall and then across the back of the sandy beach at Nesti Voe. Keep right to follow a grassy path along the coast, watching out for any resident seals, otters and eider ducks. Climb the stile in a stone wall to continue to the Point of Hovie as the cliffs start to rise. The path runs along the inside of a stone wall and then overlooks the Holm of Noss which has a large sea arch on its far side. The next section of coastline is home to some of the island's many puffins, so keep away from their burrows near the top of the cliffs.

After passing a big chunk of cliff almost detached from the main island, the route starts to climb steeply. The smell of the gannetry will probably hit you before the first views of the highest cliff, the magnificent Noup of Noss. These 180m cliffs are the highest on Shetland's east coast and are home to more than 25,000 black and white guillemots and 20,000 gannets, as well as many fulmars, shags and puffins. Nearby sand eel spawning grounds provide a source of food out to sea.

Keep climbing to reach the round trig point at the summit of the Noup of Noss. The descent path stays inside the stone

wall and passes a series of deep inlets and small headlands. The heather moorland is an important habitat for snipe, dunlin, lapwing and oystercatcher, as well as great skuas, who will protect their territories, nests and young ferociously by dive-bombing any unwary walkers – carry a stick or wave your arms above your head to deter them.

As the cliffs become much lower continue close to the coast, eventually reaching a stile in a stone wall. Climb this and immediately turn left to head inland alongside the wall. When you reach a gate on your left, turn right to follow the grassy track back to the house at the start. If you have time, the small headland of Big Ness immediately in front of the house is a great place from which to look for otters, porpoises, dolphins and even the occasional passing orca in Noss Sound.

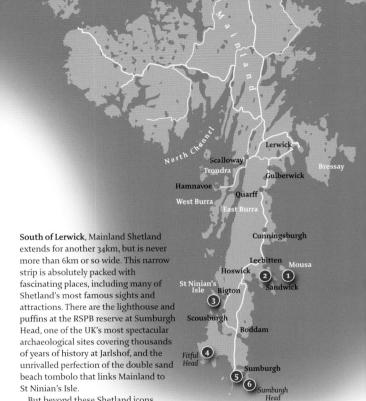

South of Lerwick, Mainland Shetland extends for another 34km, but is never more than 6km or so wide. This narrow strip is absolutely packed with fascinating places, including many of Shetland's most famous sights and attractions. There are the lighthouse and puffins at the RSPB reserve at Sumburgh Head, one of the UK's most spectacular archaeological sites covering thousands of years of history at Jarlshof, and the unrivalled perfection of the double sand beach tombolo that links Mainland to St Ninian's Isle.

But beyond these Shetland icons there are hidden delights too, including the towering cliffs falling from the moorland of Fitful Head, the many delightful headlands and promontories to explore along the eastern coastline, the Iron Age blockhouse at Ness of Burgi, as well as a whole host of brochs from the same period.

Off the east coast – across a narrow sound often visited by orca – is the island of Mousa. This is another RSPB nature reserve, but is best known for being the site of the most remarkable and best preserved broch of all.

Puffin at Sumburgh Head ▶

South Mainland and Mousa

Mousa

Distance 3.5km **Time** 2 hours
Terrain open grazing land, faint paths,
boggy in places, confined, narrow steps
inside the broch **Map** OS Explorer 466
Access Mousa boat from Sandsayre,
nearest bus stop to the pier is Sandwick
Central, buses from Lerwick

**A daytrip to Mousa by boat is a magical
experience. This walk explores this small
island nature reserve and visits the finest
of all Iron Age brochs.**

The boat to Mousa departs daily except
Saturdays from April to mid-September.
Sailing times can change with the tides
and the trip can be cancelled in poor
weather. There are also evening trips in the
summer to watch the storm petrels
returning to their roosts in the broch, but
these give less time. This walk fits with the
daytime sailings.

Before you leave Sandsayre Pier for
Mousa, make sure you visit the excellent
exhibition about the local area housed in
the old boatshed. The trip across Mousa
Sound takes you to the jetty near the
narrow pinch point which almost divides
the island in two – known as North and
South Isle. This route follows an anti-
clockwise circuit of South Isle.

Walk to the right of the building before
heading inland for a very short distance
and then turning right to cross a
boardwalk over a wet area. On the far side
go diagonally right to begin the walk along
the west coast. Once through a gap in the
fence continue round the coastline. Soon
the spectacular remains of Mousa Broch
can be seen across the bay. Pass through
gaps in two stone walls and then keep to
the boardwalk, which protects the nesting
sites of thousands of terns and storm

petrels amongst the adjacent stones.

Mousa is the best preserved example of an Iron Age broch and was thought to have been built to demonstrate power and wealth. It has a twin broch across the water, but most of its stones have been re-used for nearby buildings. The isolated position of Mousa and the island's almost limitless supply of stones has protected it from the same fate.

The broch is entered on the seaward side; torches are available from a cupboard near the entrance. A spiral staircase climbs steeply between the double-walled structure to reach the top from where there is a magnificent view over the water. Thought to have been built around 100BC, it may originally have had a wooden structure within with a number of floors and a roof supported from joists lodged in gaps in the thick walls. The broch features in the *Orkneyinga Saga* and tells of Earl Harald Maddadsson laying siege to it in 1153 following the abduction of his mother who was being held inside. Archaeologists working on the broch in 1861 found a large number of animal bones, including those of many otters, who may have taken up residence after the last humans moved out.

From the broch take the waymarked grassy path which climbs inland. Go through a gap in a dyke and keep right to head to the right of a lochan, crossing boggy and stony ground. Bear left around the back of West Pool, sticking to the waymarked route to avoid disturbing bird-nesting sites and the harbour seals which use the pool as a place to haul out and pup during the summer months.

A gap in another stone wall leads to East Pool, which also has a population of seals. Near the end of the wall bear left to follow a vague path along the east side of Mousa, sticking to the coast with occasional waymarkers. Turn inland at East Ham to follow the waterside to the point where the island is almost divided. Follow the path on the left side of a stone bank through a gap in a fence, soon returning to the building and jetty for the return boat trip.

◄ Mousa Broch

No Ness and the Broch of Burraland

Distance 8.25km **Time** 3 hours 30
Terrain minor road, track, grassy coast
with stiles, boggy and pathless in places
Map OS Explorer 466 **Access** buses from
Lerwick to Sandwick Central, 1km from
the start

**Visit the remote remains of the Iron Age
broch opposite its more famous Mousa
twin on this exploration of the quiet
No Ness peninsula.**

The walk starts from the attractive
settlement of Sandwick. There is limited
parking near the seafront – follow the sign
for No Ness and park either where the road
first reaches the coast or a short distance
further on near a picnic table. Take care to
park considerately and not block any
entrances (if necessary park further away
and walk to the start point). Walk along
the road, passing the picnic table, to leave
the houses and lovely bay behind. When
the tarmac ends continue ahead through
a gate onto a track. Follow this along the
coast, eventually going through another
gate in a large dyke with a stile adjacent.
Now leave the track where it bends left and
carry on with the coastal cliffs on your
right. Any paths here are made by sheep
and it can be wet underfoot in places; the
coastal scenery, however, is superb. Soon a
rocky hole and sea arch near the Point of
Skaag are passed and as the route goes
around a deep geo at Vins Taing, a sea cave
is visible at the foot of the cliffs.

The end of the peninsula is marked by

some concrete remains from World War II, which may have been a gun emplacement. After rounding the point follow the cliffs north up the eastern side of the peninsula, keeping to the right of a small lochan. Mousa, or 'the Mossy Isle', lies across the sound and there are some fine cliffs and impressive geos on this section of coastline. When you reach a dyke, climb the stile and continue along the coast.

Ignore the next stile on the left and aim nearer to the east coast. After two more stiles keep on the inland side of the fence, eventually moving away from the coastline and heading up higher ground over a grassy hillock, aiming to meet the next fence at another stile. From here go back downhill towards the coast, at first on the landward side, then over a stile to the seaward side of the clifftop fence. Soon you arrive at the remains of the Broch of Burraland. Although the Iron Age broch is not as well preserved as its twin across the water on Mousa, the walls still stand up to 3.5m on one side and its strategic position, protecting the narrow Sound of Mousa, can be really appreciated. A number of nearby buildings, now in a ruinous state themselves, have been created over the

years from the broch's original stones.

From the broch continue following the coastline north, eventually reaching a gate in a fence. Here you can extend the walk along the coast to Sand Lodge and the Wick of Sandsayre before returning by road, but this route aims for the track at the gate which can be seen a short distance inland. Turn right along the track and take the left fork when it branches. Just before the farm buildings turn right along the surfaced road, then when it meets the minor road, go left to return to Sandwick.

St Ninian's Isle

**Distance 5.75km Time 2 hours 30
Terrain sandy beach, grassy clifftops,
pathless and boggy in places
Map OS Explorer 466 Access occasional
feeder bus to Bigton; connects to Lerwick**

**The enticing narrow strip of sand that
connects St Ninian's Isle to Mainland is
one of Shetland's most iconic images.
Cross this tombolo to explore the
coastline of the isle, including the
remains of an ancient chapel.**

From Bigton take the signed (very)
minor road to the parking area for
St Ninian's Isle. Even on a dull day the
first glimpse of this narrow strip of sand
leading out to the island is breathtaking.
Start by passing a bench and heading
down onto the spectacular sands.

A tombolo is the name given to a narrow
spit or bar which ties an island to its larger
sibling; in Shetland such a strip of land can
also be called an ayre. In this case,

St Ninian's Isle was once a true island
before the sand tombolo formed.

Cross the sand and at the far end walk
up the sandy track. Turn left on the
springy turf to begin the clockwise circuit.
Staying on the low clifftops, the southern
tip of the island is soon reached. With
spectacular views over the rocky islets of
Coar Holm and Inns Holm, keep heading
round above the cliffs, climbing a stile over
a dyke and a second one in a fence.

Once you come to Longa Berg, at the
westernmost point of the island, the route
cuts back to round the head of a deep bay,
with views over Hich Holm and the open
ocean. Detour around the back of the deep
inlet of Selchie Geo and keep bearing north
over the short grass. The highest point of
the island, Loose Head, is also its northern
tip and is marked with a trig point. Now
follow the cliffs of the eastern side of the
island, crossing a stile at a fence and
another over a dyke. The ground can be

◀ St Ninian's Isle tombolo

boggy and the path a little indistinct in places on this section.

Eventually you reach the ruins of St Ninian's Chapel. Go through the gate to explore the 12th-century chapel. You can then peer through a grille in the ground to view the remains of a much older original chapel beneath which was the site of Shetland's oldest Christian burial. There is evidence it was used well before Christianity was brought to the islands. Ninian is thought to have been a Briton who studied in Rome and set up a religious order in Whithorn in Galloway, where he lived from around 90 to 430,

although actual accounts from that time are sketchy. He is unlikely to have visited Shetland and it is probable that the chapel was dedicated to him at a later date. It was here that the St Ninian's Hoard was discovered in 1958 by a local schoolboy taking part in an excavation of the site. An unrivalled collection of Pictish silver objects made during the second half of the 8th century, including feasting bowls, ornate cutlery, jewellery and weapons, the hoard is now in the National Museum of Scotland in Edinburgh, but you can see stunning replica artefacts in Lerwick's Shetland Museum.

Return to the start by continuing in the same direction past the chapel before picking up the sandy track back down to the beach and across the sands.

Loose Head
The Neapack
Coll Field
Ireland Wick
Scarfi Taing
Bigton
Frora Stack
Selchie Geo
Hich Holm
St Ninian's Isle
Bigton Wick
chapel (ruin)
To A970 & Lerwick
Longa Berg
Sweyn Holm
St Ninian's Bay
To A970 & Sumburgh
B9122
Coar Holm
Inns Holm

0   1km

Fitful Head

**Distance 9km Time 4 hours 30
Terrain minor road, track, rough pathless
moorland above steep, unprotected cliffs
Map OS Explorer 470 Access occasional
link bus to Quendale**

**Fitful Head is a high moorland which
drops dramatically to the sea on its
western side. With fabulous views, this
circular walk runs along the rugged rim of
great coastal cliffs, protected by skuas
during the breeding season, before
returning to Quendale.**

There is parking near Quendale Mill
which is well signed from the main road.
This is a beautifully restored watermill
with an interesting museum and café. This
walk takes an anti-clockwise circular route
across farmland to reach the coast. Start by
walking north to Hillwell, back along the

approach road. Watch out for a surfaced
track on the left next to a house (signed
Private Road and NATS).

Follow this road as it rises gently
and then dips before climbing more
steeply to emerge suddenly high above
the sea at the col between Windy Stacks
and Rushy Cups. You can either continue
on the road and rejoin the route at the
summit, or leave the road shortly after it
swings left, heading up between the
clifftops and an old quarry, to enjoy the
coastal scenery for as long as possible.

The coastal option continues over boggy
grassland above the cliffs. Fitful Head is a
Marilyn – a hill with more than 150m of
ascent on all sides – and as such attracts
some hill-baggers, but it remains pretty
quiet with sheep usually the only company
and no real walkers' paths. Great skuas are

◄ Cliffs near the summit of Fitful Head

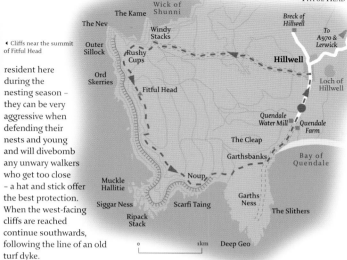

resident here during the nesting season – they can be very aggressive when defending their nests and young and will divebomb any unwary walkers who get too close – a hat and stick offer the best protection. When the west-facing cliffs are reached continue southwards, following the line of an old turf dyke.

Soon the going gets steeper again for the final push to the summit of Fitful Head, where the golfball-like enclosed radar provides coverage as part of the national air traffic control network. The trig point is just a little way beyond the building. Keep to the fenceline with the high cliffs on your right as the route starts to descend over wild heather moorland.

Further along the coast the walk passes the crash site of a World War II Lancaster bomber. The aircraft was returning from a mission to bomb the Nazi battleship *Tirpitz* in March 1942 and all seven crewmen were killed. As you continue along the clifftop you can choose to detour down to Siggar Ness, a steep and narrow peninsula, but it depends how much time and energy you have in reserve as it would be necessary to

retrace your steps right back up to the main clifftop. Otherwise you can cut across the moorland above Siggar Ness and rejoin the cliffs above the Noup from where you can see the sands of the Bay of Quendale stretching ahead.

Stay on the inland side of a fence, stepping over it when you meet another fence, and then keep dropping down the steep slope to reach the burn dividing Fitful Head from Garths Ness peninsula. Keep the fence on your right and cut across the neck of land north of Garths Ness, aiming for a gate onto a track at Garthsbanks. Turn left to follow the track back to Quendale Mill. On the way you can detour through a signed gate to visit the fine beach.

Ness of Burgi

Distance 3.25km **Time** 1 hour 30 (round trip) **Terrain** track, grassy coastline; short rocky section with handrail **Map** OS Explorer 466 **Access** buses to Scatness junction, 500m north of the start

This beautiful short walk visits the fascinating 2000-year-old ruins of a fort, crossing a narrow rocky rib to reach a remote-feeling headland.

If using the bus follow the minor road through Scatness to the turning area at the far end – if driving, park a short way back from here (not in the turning area itself) before continuing on foot along the track. As you start keep an eye open for the grain drying kiln next to the old stone house on the right-hand side. Go through a gate straight ahead when the track bends left towards a house.

Follow the grassy track, enjoying great views looking back towards Fitful Head over some ruins and scattered lochans. Leave the track when it bends left at the end of the wall and keep straight ahead on the flat grassy land leading towards the headland. The peninsula soon narrows and there is a short section over pebbles before another wider grassy section. When the land narrows dramatically use the handrail to guide your way over the rocky spine leading to the headland. From here the route becomes easier again with good views of neighbouring Sumburgh Head to the east.

Carry straight on to reach an information board giving details about the Ness of Burgi Iron Age Block House, the structure ahead on the left-hand side of the peninsula. Dating back 2000 years, this was

built at the same time as Shetland's brochs and is thought to have been a type of fort or defensive refuge, although some archaeologists believe it was built to impress rather than for an actual practical purpose. You can crawl through the narrow entrance which leads to a fine stone-built enclosure with chambers in the walls. The strategic location – at a time when most travel would have been by sea – would be hard to improve on.

From the fort it is possible to continue a short distance to the end of the headland for views of Horse Island. To return to the start, retrace the outward route.

While you're in the area it's also worth visiting Old Scatness, just up the A970 on the way to Lerwick. The Iron Age broch and village here were discovered during the construction of Sumburgh Airport's access road in the 1970s. Costumed guides lead tours of the site on certain days during summer and booking must be made well in advance.

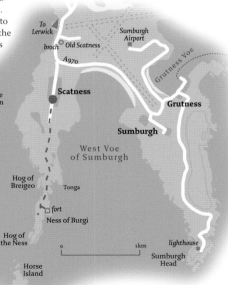

◀ Sumburgh Head seen from the Ness of Burgi

Sumburgh Head and Jarlshof

Distance 5.5km **Time** 3 hours
Terrain coastal paths with stiles, rough
in places, minor road **Map** OS Explorer 466
Access bus from Lerwick to Sumburgh

**Combine two of Shetland's most popular
attractions on this wonderful coastal
circuit. It starts at the amazing remains of
Jarlshof before heading along increasingly
impressive cliffs to Sumburgh Head with
its lighthouse and puffins.**

Start from the Jarlshof Car Park which is
behind the Sumburgh Hotel. Take the
grassy path towards Jarlshof between the
fence and stone wall. It is well worth
visiting the Jarlshof complex (entry
charge) which begins with the remains of a
16th-century mansion but then leads on to
much older and well-preserved Viking, Iron
Age, Bronze Age and Stone Age houses –

one of the UK's richest archaeological sites.

From the Jarlshof entrance, go through a
gate signed for the coastal path and walk
with the sea on your right, heading
towards Sumburgh Head which is visible
in the distance. Cross a number of stiles as
the path continues, marked with cairns in
places. As the lighthouse grows nearer
climb a further stile and follow the path
which climbs on the landward side of the
dyke, soon reaching another stile.
Eventually aim left through a gap and turn
right to follow the path towards the
lighthouse. There are a couple of viewing
points overlooking puffin burrows at the
top of the cliffs – often with their owners
parading outside during the summer
breeding season.

There is a charge to visit the lighthouse
complex, which includes an interesting

marine life centre with live cameras trained on the nearby seabirds. There are fascinating exhibits on the life of the lighthouse and its keepers, including its role during World War II. There is also a panoramic café, a disused foghorn, with views to Fair Isle on a clear day, and numerous places to watch the birds from the landward side of the lighthouse boundary walls.

The cliffs of the headland are home to large colonies of fulmars, razorbills, guillemots, kittiwakes and puffins and the noise can be almost overwhelming during the nesting season. The paths around the centre allow you to get very close to the birds in places without overly disturbing them. Once you have seen enough, head back down the road, passing a model whale, to reach a parking area and a much smaller lighthouse.

From the car park go through a gap in the wall and climb the grassy slope of Compass Hill, keeping near to the cliffs on the right. Once the gradient eases off it's a short walk to the summit. Pass between the radar station buildings and continue in the same direction to descend towards Grutness. From here you can see the planes at Sumburgh Airport below; sometimes the main road is closed to allow the full

runway to be used. Carry on, staying near the cliffs until you reach a gap in the stone wall at the bottom of the hill.

Turn left to join the road at a bend and go right to reach the cluster of houses at Grutness. The pier (from where the ferry to Fair Isle departs) is a short detour to the right, but the walk continues left along the A970. Ignore the turn on the right for the airport and take the next left to reach the Sumburgh Hotel and the start.

◄ Looking back at Jarlshof

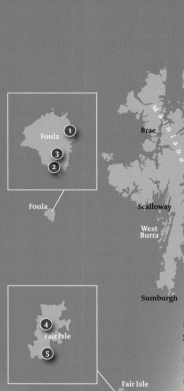

Foula

Fair Isle

Foula and Fair Isle are the most remote inhabited islands in Britain. A visit to either requires advance planning and is dependent on the weather, but whether you travel by air or sea the experience is unlikely to be forgotten.

Despite its location Fair Isle is well known – both for its knitwear and for its hallowed status amongst birdwatchers as a place to spot rare migrants. It is set almost equidistant between Sumburgh Head on Mainland Shetland and North Ronaldsay, the northernmost island of the Orkney archipelago (around 40km from each), and has a community of 60 people. This tiny island actually packs in a wide variety of scenery, with towering sea cliffs and wild moors rising up to Ward Hill, and verdant green fields, too.

Foula, set out around 23km west of Mainland, has a population of around 30 scattered over the eastern part of the island, whilst across the other side a range of sculpted hills sweep up to Da Sneug and then fall in a series of huge cliffs to the Atlantic Ocean. At Da Kame the cliffs reach 376m – second only to those on St Kilda as the highest in the UK. Swooping over the moors of both islands are vast colonies of aggressive skuas, defending their nests from walkers, whilst puffins and other seabirds can be found all around the coastline.

Shetland pony, Foula ▶

Foula and Fair Isle

Foula coastal walk

Distance 4km **Time** 2 hours 30
Terrain very wet and pathless to start,
easier coastal walking with stiles, minor
road **Map** OS Explorer 467 **Access** air and
ferry service from Mainland Shetland

**A slice of remote island life away from the
rugged hills, this coastal circuit explores
the east coast of Foula between the
airstrip and the ferry pier, with plenty of
opportunities for watching Shetland
ponies and nesting puffins along the way.**

To reach one of Britain's most remote
inhabited islands is an adventure in itself.
Day visits by air are possible with advance
booking from Tingwall, but the weather
means the flights are only confirmed
minutes before departure. The Foula
passenger ferry runs three times a week

from Walls during the summer months –
again booking is essential and the trip of
two hours and 15 minutes is very weather
dependent; a rough crossing may be
enlivened with dolphins or whales. As the
boat is based on Foula it is not possible to
make a daytrip by sea.

This walk is described from Foula airstrip
but can also be picked up at the ferry pier.
The population of Foula declined during
the 19th and 20th centuries, with a
dramatic fall after the loss of the regular
mailboat *Lass* in 1962. However, the
remaining residents were determined to
keep their community going and built the
airstrip themselves in the late 1970s. Today
the population stands at around 30. Wait
for any planes to depart before heading
round the northern end of the runway and

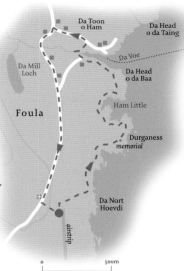

crossing a stretch of extremely boggy pathless ground to reach the coastal cliffs to the east.

Turn left along the clifftops, going through a signed gate to reach the war memorial. At the time of World War I around 100 people lived on Foula and six of the island's young men were lost in the conflict. Continue along the cliffs, rounding the bay of Ham Little. During the summer months watch out for puffins, which nest in burrows at the top of the cliffs. Cross a couple of wooden boardwalks and pass through another walkers' gate to go round the far side of the bay.

Once past Da Head o da Baa, Foula's main jetty comes into view across Da Voe with the 12-seater ferry, the *New Advance*, usually hauled out of the water for safety at this, the only sheltered spot on the island's coast. Follow a marker post inland, aiming for a house on the south side of Da Voe and, after going through a gate, turn immediately right on a footpath that leads down towards a footbridge over the burn.

Cross the bridge and climb the broad path on the far side, passing a garden sheltered by stone walls, to reach a road. The jetty is a short detour to the right, but this route turns left. At the T-junction turn left along Foula's main road to return towards the airstrip.

A reminder of Foula's isolated position remains in the date that islanders have traditionally celebrated Christmas. When the rest of Britain adopted the Gregorian calendar in 1752, Foula remained on the Julian calendar. It kept 1800 as a leap year but had changed to the Gregorian by 1900, when it did not observe a leap year. The result is that Foula still traditionally celebrates Christmas Day on 6 January and New Year on the 13th, so it could be the perfect place to escape the festive mayhem.

Eventually the road passes the Baxter Chapel on the right. Although still a working chapel it has a room full of fascinating photographs and information about the island. From here continue on the road, taking the next left to return to the airstrip which has a tiny waiting room and toilet.

◀ The *New Advance* hauled out at Foula's jetty

Da Sneck Ida Smaalie

**Distance 5km Time 2 hours 30
Terrain indistinct and very boggy path,
navigation skills needed
Map OS Explorer 467 Access air and ferry
service from Mainland Shetland**

**Venture into the heartland of Foula to
reach an amazing 30m-deep split in the
earth known as Da Sneck Ida Smaalie on
the island's western cliffs. This out-and-
back walk also passes through a dramatic
glen nestled between imposing hills.**

Foula is usually reached by air, which
allows for daytrips on certain days of the
week – booking is essential and take-off is
never guaranteed until the last moment.
After enjoying amazing views from the
tiny plane, start the walk from the
airstrip, heading towards the island's main
road. When the T-junction with the
island's main road is reached, cross and
bear right, then aim for the Baxter Chapel
almost opposite. Whilst it still functions
as a chapel it also houses a welcoming
room for visitors, crammed full of
information and photographs
documenting life on Foula.

From the chapel bear southwest
diagonally inland, keeping almost parallel
to the road at first, to reach a circular stone
enclosure. This is the remains of a
planticrub, used to shelter and grow kail
and other animal fodder, usually fertilised
with seaweed.

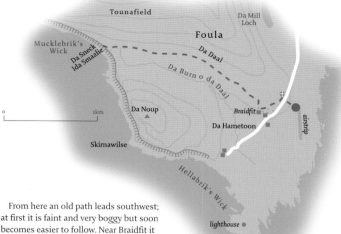

From here an old path leads southwest; at first it is faint and very boggy but soon becomes easier to follow. Near Braidfit it joins a broader path marked by stones on each side. This path heads north and then northwest into Da Daal, the broad glen dividing Foula's main hills and Da simply being the local dialect for 'the'. At times the path disappears but keep going along the northern flank of Da Daal. After a rougher stretch, the ground becomes grassier underfoot as the highest point of Da Daal is approached. From here, cross flatter grassy terrain towards the west coast of Foula, keeping to the bottom of the steep slopes to the right.

As you near the coast look out for the top of Da Sneck Ida Smaalie, a narrow, deep, vertically-sided rock cleft formed by a landslide. When seen from the sea it splits the great western cliffs of the island almost right down to their base. Although you can peer into the dank and ferny depths, do not attempt to descend into the Sneck as it requires proper climbing equipment, experience and a guide; safe to say this is one place that you'd get into more easily than you'd ever get back out! You can, however, explore the flat grassy ground on either side of Da Sneck and enjoy the sea views. Looking south along the coast, the great hill and cliff of Da Noup rises very impressively – those with lots of energy could aim to climb it, though the ascent is very steep and care must be taken not to get too near the edge. Look out for puffins which have burrows on the grassy ground above the cliffs.

The return route is a simple retracing of the outward walk through Da Daal to the airstrip.

◀ Da Noup

Da Sneug

**Distance 6.75km Time 3 hours 30
Terrain pathless exposed moorland,
navigation skills needed
Map OS Explorer 470 Access air and
ferry service from Mainland Shetland**

**Climb to the summit of the highest hill on
Foula for an unforgettable view over this
remote isle. During the summer months
you will share the hill with great skuas as
the island is home to the world's largest
colony. They compete fiercely for breeding
territory with Arctic skuas, known locally
as 'skootie allens'.**

Starting from Foula airstrip, head along
the access road – the ridge climbed en
route to the summit is in view directly
ahead. At the junction with the island's
main road, go straight across and aim for

the Baxter Chapel just to the right. As well
as the delightful small chapel there is a
room which acts as Foula's visitor centre.

From the chapel aim northwest across
the pathless land to reach the start of the
ridge. Here you'll see numerous circular
stone enclosures called planticrubs
scattered across the unpromising land.
These were once productive fertilised
patches growing kail and other crops
sheltered from the winds. As you climb the
ridge of Bodlifield, keep aiming for the first
summit, Hamnafield, the name a reminder
of the island's strong Norse connections.

Once the summit of Hamnafield is
reached the main steep climb of the day is
behind you, and the lovely curved ridge
leading to the top of Da Sneug can be seen
ahead. Descend slightly before continuing

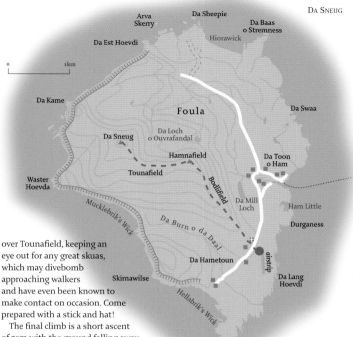

Arva Skerry

Da Sheepie

Da Baas o Stremness

Hiorawick

Da Est Hoevdi

0   1km

Foula

Da Kame

Da Swaa

Da Loch o Ouvrafandal

Da Sneug

Hamnafield

Da Toon o Ham

Tounafield

Bodlifield

Da Mill Loch

Ham Little

Waster Hoevda

Mucklebrik's Wick

Da Burn o da Daal

Durganess

over Tounafield, keeping an eye out for any great skuas, which may divebomb approaching walkers and have even been known to make contact on occasion. Come prepared with a stick and hat!

Da Hametoun

airstrip

Skirnawilse

Da Lang Hoevdi

Hellabrik's Wick

Nessaskerry

The final climb is a short ascent of 70m with the ground falling away steeply to your right. Just before the top, you pass the Brethren standing stones. Little is known about their origin, but it is thought they date back to prehistoric times. Da Sneug's summit is topped by a large cairn and trig point and has an amazing view over the whole of Foula. In clear conditions Shetland's Westside and Papa Stour can be seen almost 50km away, the vast expanse of water in between emphasising Foula's remoteness.

It is possible to descend southwards from the bealach below Tounafield into Da

Daal and then follow a faint path through the glen to visit Da Sneck Ida Smaalie before returning on the Da Daal path back to the airstrip. However, this would add at least a couple of hours to the overall time and the route down is very rough and pathless with tussocky terrain underfoot. The easiest return route is simply to follow the outward route back with views down to the sheep which nonchalantly take over Foula's runway between flights.

◀ Brethren standing stones

Ward Hill of Fair Isle

Distance **4.25km** Time **3 hours**
Terrain **track, path, pathless section near
high unprotected cliffs, navigation skills
needed** Map **OS Explorer 470** Access **air and
ferry service from Mainland Shetland**

**A climb to the top of Ward Hill brings you
to the highest summit on one of Britain's
most isolated islands where you can truly
appreciate the remote location. The return
route passes spectacular cliff scenery.**

There is a regular air service from
Tingwall to Fair Isle – the experience of
flying low over Mainland Shetland and the
sea approach to Fair Isle seen from an
eight-seater aeroplane is extremely
memorable. In good weather the MV *Good
Shepherd* provides a wonderful two and a
half hour sea journey to the island's
natural sheltered harbour, North Haven,
conveniently near the Bird Observatory,
where many visitors choose to stay.
Flights are often very busy so booking
well in advance in the summer months
is advisable as is the ability to be flexible
as flights and ferries are often disrupted
by bad weather.

This walk starts from the Fair Isle
airstrip, easily reached along the island's
arterial road from the ferry jetty or Bird
Observatory. After waiting for any planes
to depart – and checking there are none
coming in – cross the runway to a track on
the far side which leads uphill towards a
cluster of telecommunications masts. The
climb on the track is straightforward, but
the ever-improving views south give good
reason to stop and admire the island
stretching away to the lighthouse and
Malcolm's Point.

The end of the track is reached at a
series of old concrete huts beyond the
telecoms mast. Here a rough path aims
steeply uphill for the final climb to the

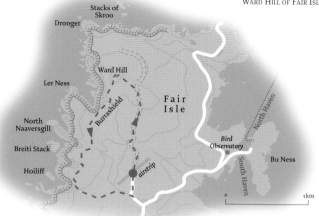

true summit, which is marked with a trig point and cairn. There is also a lot of concrete debris left over from the RAF radar station that operated here for the duration of World War II. The collapsed remains of the radar tower and its motor can still be seen, but nothing is visible of the railway that was built to transport equipment from the lower base to the station on Ward Hill. It was protected by machine gun emplacements on site as well as two anti-aircraft batteries located at each end of the island.

The views on a clear day provide a peaceful antidote to the concrete wreckage of war. Sumburgh Head at the southern tip of Shetland's Mainland can be made out in good weather, as well as the lighthouse on North Ronaldsay, the most northerly island of the Orkney archipelago.

Although you can return back down the track, this would avoid seeing any of Fair Isle's best scenic feature, its impressive coastline. So bear south over pathless ground to reach the wild cliffs of the west coast. Keeping safely back from the clifftop, head around a deep geo where a gannet colony can be seen far below. Cut across the next headland before descending to pass round another geo.

A short climb leads up to Burrashield, after which you follow the coast, passing two more geos with natural arches and stacks to enjoy. At the second geo turn left to follow a substantial drystane dyke inland, keeping on the near side of the wall. After a short distance you come to an enclosure; from here bear ENE aiming for the end of the airstrip. Before approaching the runway keep right to reach the access road, then turn left to return to the terminal building – which bears little resemblance to what you'd normally find at an airport.

◀ Summit of Ward Hill

Malcolm's Head and Sheep Rock

Distance 12.75km **Time** 5 hours 30
Terrain minor road, fields, stiles, pathless
coast, boggy in places, grazing land
(dogs to be kept under tight control)
Map OS Explorer 470 **Access** air and ferry
service from Mainland Shetland

**Birds and coastal scenery, together with
an enthusiasm for knitwear, are reasons
that many choose to visit Fair Isle. This
walk takes in the best of the stunning
coastline with many opportunities for
birdwatching along the way.**

The walk starts from the airstrip, but if
setting out from the jetty at North Haven
or the Bird Observatory just follow the
road south to join the route. From the
airstrip take the road downhill, passing a
large bird trap used by the observatory for
research on migratory birds. At the
junction just beyond, turn right and
continue as the high dome of Malcolm's
Head comes into view in the distance.

Continue past the doctor's surgery and
keep right where the road forks for the
shop. Just before the shop is reached and
soon after the road bends left, climb a stile
on the right and aim straight across the
field towards the coast.

Another stile leads to the cliff edge
where a stunning view of Hundi Stack is
revealed by just a short detour to the right.
However, this route goes south to follow
the coast in an anti-clockwise direction
with the first objective to climb the first of
the three headlands. Bear left over a stile
and go directly up the steep slope to reach
the top. Here a high sea stack can be seen,
as well as sheer-sided Fogli Stack just
beyond Malcolm's Head. Drop down the far
side of the small headland and over two
stiles and through a gate to pass a fin-
shaped sea stack. Cross two further stiles
before climbing Malcolm's Head, where an
old coastguard lookout marks the top.

Descend close to the cliffs and detour to

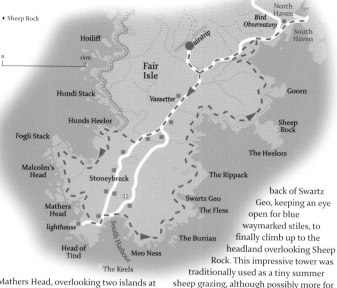

◀ Sheep Rock

North Haven

Bird Observatory

South Haven

Hoiliff

airstrip

Fair Isle

Goorn

Hundi Stack

Vaasetter

Hunds Heelor

Sheep Rock

Fogli Stack

The Heelors

Malcolm's Head

Stoneybreck

The Rippack

Mathers Head

Swartz Geo

lighthouse

The Fless

Head of Tind

South Harbour

Meo Ness

The Burrian

The Keels

0   1km

Mathers Head, overlooking two islands at Black Holm where puffins can be seen in the summer months. A stile leads to the back of a deep inlet with another stile on the far side, the route keeping close to the coast until you reach a stile just before the road. Turn left away from the south lighthouse, then left again after The Puffin (where National Trust for Scotland volunteers stay) to cross the cattle grid. Take the next right, just after the cemetery. Before the white house cross a stile on the right to follow the coast. Another stile leads to open ground and the route climbs along the cliff edge, crossing stiles where necessary and eventually reaching the headland. Continue and head round the

back of Swartz Geo, keeping an eye open for blue waymarked stiles, to finally climb up to the headland overlooking Sheep Rock. This impressive tower was traditionally used as a tiny summer sheep grazing, although possibly more for the adventure of hauling the sheep up by rope from boats than for any lack of grazing on the main island.

Carry on north along the cliffs, diverting inland almost to the road to cross the top of a deep ravine where the remains of a grain mill and a bird trap can be seen. Turn right at the road and pass the Bird Observatory (where visitors are welcome and refreshments are available) to reach the sandy beach at North Haven where Fair Isle's ferry berths. From here the return to the airstrip is back along the road, taking a shortcut on the left next to a bird trap and turning right after the information board to climb up to the start.

Index